Youth Clubs

Association, Participation, Friendship and Fun!

Sue Robertson

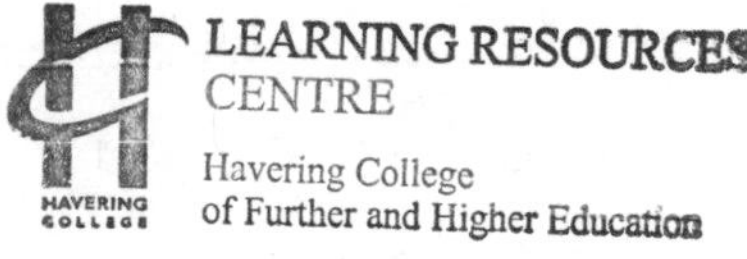

Russell House Publishing

First published in 2005 by:
Russell House Publishing Ltd.
4 St. George's House
Uplyme Road
Lyme Regis
Dorset DT7 3LS

Tel: 01297-443948
Fax: 01297-442722
e-mail: help@russellhouse.co.uk
www.russellhouse.co.uk

British Library Cataloguing-in-publication Data:

A catalogue record for this book is available from the British Library.

ISBN: 1-903855-38-1

Typeset by TW Typesetting, Plymouth, Devon
Printed by Cromwell Press, Trowbridge

About Russell House Publishing

RHP is a group of social work, probation, education and youth and community work practitioners and academics working in collaboration with a professional publishing team.
Our aim is to work closely with the field to produce innovative and valuable materials to help managers, trainers, practitioners and students.
We are keen to receive feedback on publications and new ideas for future projects.
For details of our other publications please visit our website or ask us for a catalogue. Contact details are on this page.

Contents

Dedication

This book is dedicated to all the friends I have made through my youth work – you know who you are!

About the author

Sue Robertson has been a youth worker since 1978 when she started to help out in her village youth club in Devon. This led her on to full-time club work in Devon and Cheshire. In the late 1980s she worked on a project involving young people with disabilities in the youth service in Ealing, and later became a youth advisor in Croydon, involved in management and service development. The early 1990s saw a family move to Gloucestershire, involvement in part-time club work, and managing a Youth Action Scheme. Sue set up a youth club in her village and began teaching on the youth work training course at the University of the West of England.

She is currently the Programme and Fieldwork Co-ordinator for the Diploma in Youth and Community Work at University College, Chichester, encouraging students to get involved in work in youth clubs.

Introduction

On any weekday night, throughout the country, young people gather together in youth clubs to meet each other, to chat, to do activities, to work on projects, to go on trips, to play games, and to discuss issues.

Youth clubs come under the banner of the 'youth service' which also includes detached youth work, school based projects and many other varieties of work with young people plus voluntary groups such as Scouts, Sea Cadets and the Woodcraft Folk.

What are youth clubs?

Youth clubs have been in existence in Britain since the early 1800s and provide a place for young people, from the age of 11 to 18 (priority given to those aged 14 plus) to meet and take part in activities. This book focuses on general mixed clubs, i.e. clubs that are open to any young person of any religious persuasion or ethnic background. They range from the large clubs run by local authorities or voluntary associations (usually with funding from the local authority and employing paid staff) to the one night a week clubs run by volunteers in draughty church or village halls. In the Albermarle Report of 1960 (Ministry of Education) the fundamental task of the youth service was described as 'encouraging young people to come together in groups of their own choosing'. This was the high point for youth clubs as, resulting from the report, there was a massive building programme and new premises for youth clubs were built all over the country. However, nowadays, the decline of these valuable community assets is evident countrywide: the lack of new buildings provided for young people over the last 30 years stands in dramatic contrast to the makeovers of large numbers of pubs targeting a young clientele.

Nonetheless, clubs are still in business.

What goes on in clubs?

In 1961 a typical club (Ministry of Education, 1961) was open five nights a week with the occasional additional activities on Saturday or Sunday. The young people were grouped by age (14–16 and 17–21) and there were 450 members on the books with an average attendance of 100. Activities included film shows, dancing, drama, hairdressing, football, judo, photography, woodwork, radio and model making, canoe and boat building and motor cycle repairs plus the Duke of Edinburgh Award Scheme. When Withywood Youth Club opened in 1962 it was open from 9 in the morning six days a week! (Sharpe, 2004).

In the 1980s I worked in a club that opened four nights a week for the seniors (over 13s) and one night for the juniors (10–13s) as well as having an after school club for the 5–10s once a week and a couple of daytime sessions for unemployed young people. Weekend activities would happen on occasional Saturday nights and Sunday afternoons. Activities included pool, table tennis, football, art and crafts (including pottery), dancing, cinema trips, TV watching, drama, as well as outdoor activities such as camping, hill walking, canoeing and sailing. Normal week night attendance was between 20 and 50: with many more for big events or disco nights.

Today, Brighton Youth Centre is open 3 nights a week for seniors (over 12s) and Saturday morning plus an evening for under 12s. They run discos and special events on Fridays and there is also a youth club for deaf young people. They advertise a full size snooker table and Sky TV, plus art projects, pool and table tennis.

Southmead Youth Centre in Bristol is open for six hours every weekday from after school till 10pm. Within these six hours there is general social activity; youth work support, a time-tabled programme of activities and advice sessions from Connexions and the local drugs project.

At every session there is access to:

- social space
- the Internet
- tea, coffee and water
- TV
- music
- youth worker support

Regular activities include:

- computer club
- poetry/writing club
- art club
- weights training
- keep fit
- basketball
- DJ workshop
- video making and animation

Other activities take place at weekends, such as motocross training and competitions and girls' and boys' football training.

In addition to the basic programme the young people get involved in local, regional and national sports competitions, annual events such as a presentation evening, summer activities, residentials, arts projects and school holiday activities (dependent on funding).

Other events and outings arise out of discussions with the young people (Southmead Locality Plan, 2003).

Clubs like this are open all over the country night after night, although not all will have so many facilities or resources. In fact many so called full-time clubs are only open two nights a week for generic youth work (one local authority in Merton's (2005) research uses 147 buildings but over a quarter are open for less than five hours a week), but all will be working with young people who have chosen to attend.

A service in decline?

A recent survey (White, 2003) showed that 150 youth services used a total of 3,411 premises. Of these, 2,421 were owned by the local authority, (about half of which were exclusively used for youth service purposes and half were shared with other users). The remaining buildings were leased or rented. This figure does not include the hundreds of voluntary youth clubs run by churches or other faith clubs who meet in their own or rented premises.

The Youth Service Audit (Marken and Perret, 1998) described the basic youth service infrastructure as 'the foundation of open, non-stigmatising access from which specific project work with particular groups can develop'. This is club work and yet in the 1990s enthusiasm for club work seemed at an all time low, and a DfEE publication *Moving on Up* (1999) focusing on youth work, had no examples of club based work. This was in stark contrast to the 1987 DES publication, *Effective Youth Work*, which looked at the work being done in settings where young people meet, and is full of examples of centre based work and is one of the last government reports to promote open youth work (www.infed.org.uk). Nowadays, articles in *Young People Now* rarely describe the type of youth work occurring in hundreds of centres all over the country every evening. The idea that the community should provide a place for young people to meet that is safe and warm, where they can associate, try out new activities and learn new skills, relate to adults, obtain advice and information, and run things for themselves is a good one, as I demonstrate in these pages. So where have we gone wrong? Why are many youth club buildings decaying? Why are many clubs closed most of the week, and in the school holidays?

Contributory factors

There are many social and economic factors which have encouraged young people to stay at home rather than go to youth clubs. For example, central heating is now common in the home so young people gather together in each other's homes and spend time watching TV or playing the wide variety of computer games that are now available. There are many fears about safety on the streets at night and young people chat online keeping networks going without the need for physical presence. Some teachers even positively discourage attendance at clubs: one head teacher, at the beginning of the new school term, asked the question 'Are they really your friends if they want you to go out in the evening when you should be doing your homework?'

The failure to provide clubs with adequate staff and equipment and the lack of management enthusiasm have helped the decline in the significance of the youth club. The National Youth Agency, for example, may discuss youth work generically but often places more emphasis on specialist projects that are more easily evaluated. Many local authorities now describe their youth work provision as 'youth projects' instead of 'youth clubs' or 'youth centres'. Even the National Association (originally of youth clubs) has now changed its name from Youth Clubs UK to UK Youth, and many of its local associations provide little support to clubs, being providers of youth training, and supporting initiatives such as the Prince's Trust.

The recent trend to funding by bidding, of which the Youth Action Scheme (France and Wiles, 1997) was an early example, means that authorities have gone for short-term project funding. There has been no capital money for new buildings and very little for repairs and maintenance, so that youth club buildings have often fallen into disrepair and decay, or sometimes even been sold off for development.

Working as a full-time worker in a youth club is hard work and demands a big commitment and work at anti-social hours. This may explain why it is difficult to recruit staff and why club work is often seen as an unattractive placement by youth work students (who usually have to do part-time work to survive at college). As local authorities have demanded more and more from full-time workers, it is not surprising that many become 'kippered' (Ingram and Harris, 2001) meaning that the youth worker who started off as a well rounded person gets squashed flat like a kipper!

Making a case for youth clubs

Youth clubs have been part of my life for a long time, I can never hear the Sex Pistol's *Anarchy in the UK* without remembering Dale playing it, over and over, night after night, in the youth club in Exeter. I have spent some of the best times of my life in youth clubs, or on trips away with young people from the club, but also some of the worst! I remain an enthusiast for club based work, and hope this book will convince others of its enduring relevance and potential.

This book is a reference and resource book about youth clubs which makes a case for them and celebrates the daily grind and joy of youth club work. It attempts to cover the history and practice of youth work in youth clubs and draws heavily on sources from the 1800s to the present day which describe youth club work, plus my own experience as a youth club worker. It does not set out to be a 'how to' book, but aims to furnish the reader with arguments to support the continuance and development of the work, and to inspire them to get involved in a very worthwhile type of work. Youth clubs provide a valuable service to young people, and hopefully will continue to thrive in the 21st century.

Chapter 1 discusses why our communities need youth clubs and what young people get from them.

Chapter 2 offers an overview of the history of clubs, which will hopefully encourage further reading, especially of the original texts which give a fascinating picture of youth club life.

Chapter 3 looks at the roles of the adults in a youth club; the full-time and part-time workers, the volunteers and the senior club members and how they influence young people.

Chapter 4 discusses good practice in centre based work, the youth work that goes on in youth clubs, the need to make relationships and engage in informal education and how workers should go about this. It also includes a brief review of books about youth clubs.

Chapter 5 looks at issues of equal opportunity, past and present, and how to make the youth club available to all young people.

Chapter 6 examines the management and organisation of youth club work: management is an important part of achieving good practice.

Chapter 7 looks at the youth club in its community, school based and rural youth work and the importance of inter-agency work.

Chapter 8, the concluding chapter, explores how the argument for youth clubs can be made by looking at current policy ideas in the area of social exclusion and social capital. It looks to the future for youth clubs in the context of recent policy initiatives.

Chapter 1

Why Youth Clubs?

This chapter examines the arguments for youth clubs, both from the perspective of young people and society.

Association

In her 1943 book about youth clubs Josephine Brew explained how clubs met the basic human needs for companionship and to make friends. She felt that individuals created clubs 'to make friends and to maintain contact with those of like interests' Brew (1943). Human beings needed small groups, rather than large crowds. This is the distinction between association and gregariousness as described in the 19th century novel *Sybil* (Disraeli, 1845). Disraeli defines association as 'a community of purpose' and he bemoans the disappearance of it in industrial society, as without it 'men may be drawn into contiguity, but they still continue virtually isolated'.

Companionship is a pleasurable experience of group interaction associated with leisure activity; young people experience a sense of belonging, acceptance, solidarity and social affirmation simply from being together.

Association was strongly articulated as a value for the youth service in the Albermarle Report (Ministry of Education, 1960). Smith (2001) feels it is relevant today, and defines association as 'joining together in companionship to undertake some task, and the educative power of playing ones part in a group or association' and he feels that there is a need to 're-embrace the notion of the club'. Smith examines Putnam's (2000) work on Social Capital, see Chapter 8, which supports the case in favour of generic work involving the whole community and opposes concentrating resources on young people presenting problems.

The needs of young people

Surveys conducted in 1994 in Tewkesbury (Ballard and Wright, 1995), in Wales (Williamson et al., 1997) and by the DfE (1995) asking young people why they attend youth clubs, came up with similar findings, as did local questionnaires conducted by LEAs (Croydon, Bristol and Gloucestershire Youth Service Questionnaires, annual data collection) and research in

Nottingham in 2004 for the DfES (Merton et al., 2005) on the impact of youth work.

> *A place to have fun, to meet friends, talk with your mates and just mellow out, to get away from schoolwork and parents, a place where you are given a chance.*
>
> Research by Brunel University for the National Association of Clubs for Young People (2004)

Two thirds of the young people in the Impact of Youth Work survey (Merton et al., 2005) reported that youth work had made a difference to their lives – including increasing their confidence, making new friends; learning new skills, and being more able to ask for help and advice.

It is important that young people enjoy being young and youth clubs can make that time more enjoyable for many young people. As one youth worker said to me, 'we should not always see youth as a stage to be got through or a preparation for later life, but as a valuable time in itself'. Youth clubs enable young people to learn useful skills that they can use immediately, such as at Radio Southmead where young people learnt how to run a radio station, or DJ courses where young people run the club disco.

In his research in Wales, Williamson (1997) identified four needs expressed by the young people, over 15 whom he interviewed:

- The need for association – somewhere to go.
- Activities – something to do.
- Advice – someone to talk to.
- Autonomy – space of their own.

The Youth club was valued, firstly as a social meeting place, warm and friendly, and secondly for things to do including trips away, activities, special projects, discussions and issue based work. Young people also appreciated the opportunity to participate 'to have a say, if we want to'.

Somewhere to go

Much recent research, particularly concerning regeneration, gives a high priority to affordable, accessible and appropriate leisure facilities (an example is *Urban Regeneration: Responding to Young Peoples' Needs*, Joseph Rowntree Foundation, 2003). This reflects the perennial complaint from young people 'there's nothing to do around here'. A recent consultation with young people asked them what they would change for children and young people, if they could be Minister of Youth for the day (www.cypu.gov.uk/consultationresults).

Figure 1.1 shows the five most popular responses:

Comments included:

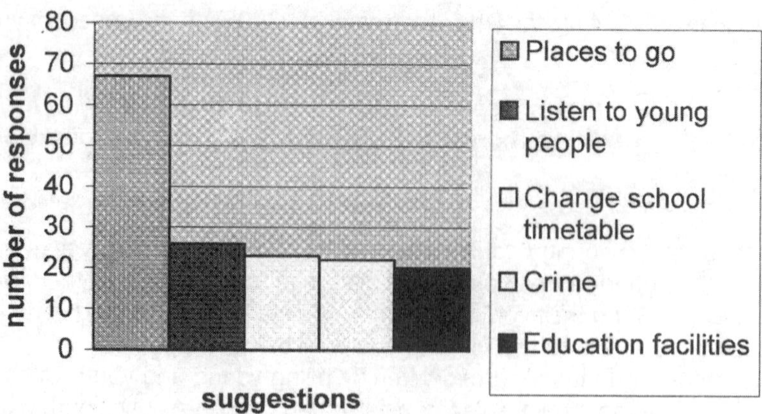

Figure 1.1

> *I would change everything like more places for teenagers to go, make prices for ice skating, swimming and bowling etc. cheaper, then they would have somewhere to go.*
>
> (Laura, 14)
>
> *I would get more hang out places and clubs for young teens.*
>
> (Liam, 13)
>
> *Leisure is important because you can do what you want to do and there isn't a teacher telling you what you can and can't do.*
>
> (Tim, 13)
>
> *Safe, friendly places should be available for teenagers to chill out together – like pubs for under 18 year olds (but no alcohol or smoke).*
>
> (Kirstie, 17)

These types of responses come up whenever young people are asked what they need in their areas. The Listen Up Report (2000) from the Home Office found that young men in particular were asking for a safe place to go to get advice and 'be themselves'.

Thirty per cent of young people surveyed on a Bristol estate in 1998 felt unsafe and wanted safe places to go (Brent, 2001). Research conducted by MORI and BMRB for the Make Space organisation (www.makespace.org.uk) found that 70 per cent of 11–16 year olds believe young people commit crime because there is not enough for them to do. One idea was:

> *To set up a young people's centre in every borough where young people can receive counselling advice, a place where they can do their homework and feel relaxed, and generally have somewhere that isn't as stressful as being at home or school.*

Research undertaken by Thomas (2003) in Oldham and by Edwards and Hatch (2003) in Coventry garnered similar comments:

> *We need a good youth club . . . to keep the boys off the street . . . we hang out on the street, smoking, and bored because there is no youth club.*
>
> (Thomas, 2003)

> *They hang around drinking because they've got nothing else to do.*
>
> (Edwards and Hatch, 2003)

Young people in the Impact of Youth Work survey (Merton et al., 2005) were generally satisfied with their youth workers but not with the state of the buildings or the opening hours (p149). The demand for youth facilities nationally is not confined to young people; local community consultations consistently place youth facilities high on the list. A survey by MORI and the Audit Commission found that 'activities for teenagers came top of the list of improvements most needed in people's local area' (Edwards and Hatch, 2003). There is a general consensus that there are too few facilities, and those that exist are often rundown and inadequate:

> *The young people in the area have little to do in the evening, and not just in the evenings, but at the weekends too. We have the facilities here for a youth club and many other facilities but I don't think they are being used to their potential.*
>
> (Older resident, quoted in Edwards and Hatch, 2003)

> *A generation of youngsters with nothing to do and nowhere to go in the evening has been created.*
>
> (Commission for Race Equality, *Young People Now*, July 2000: 5)

Recent research by the National Centre for Social Research (YPN 1–7th Sept. 2004) found that only one in five young people had visited a youth club or religious group in the past 6 months, perhaps because there are less of them to go to? At the time of the *Young People's Participation in the Youth Service* survey (DfE, 1995) 30 per cent of young people were accessing youth provision at any one time, while 60 per cent had done so at some time, this represented about six million young people. About equal numbers attended youth clubs and voluntary groups, but there were more young people from manual backgrounds in clubs. Only a handful were involved in projects or other youth service activities, so that the conclusions of this survey were really about clubs.

Again the same phrases come up – somewhere to go, to meet friends, have fun, do interesting activities and also to play a part in the community and to feel more confident. These young people are also involved in other things to a greater extent than others 'a higher proportion of youth service participants are involved in sports, arts or voluntary work than non-participants'. These findings are echoed by Gauthier and Furstenberg's research (2001) that in those countries where the state invested more in cultural and sporting facilities, young people responded by investing more of their own time in such activities. Getting young people involved is the first step; attendance can be initial evidence of success with disaffected young people (DfEE, 2000). Young people involved in a discussion at a New Deal event in Bristol wanted the youth service to offer:

> *A better place to go to, more equipment, more day time opening, teach practical skills, spend money on us, more workers.*

Instead, local authorities often try to provide a service cheaply, by erecting a temporary building or 'pod'. This would be better than nothing, but often deciding where to site it causes problems, since adults often don't want it on their patch.

A National Association of Youth Clubs publication, written for people setting up youth clubs, suggests that the work is about helping young people to create a setting where they can grow to social maturity. As young people have limited opportunities to socialise outside school, youth clubs offer a place which is 'really their own'. They have facilities, a programme of events, a base from which to go out, a chance to try new things and explore important issues, and an opportunity to make informal relationships with adults and other young people (Myhill, 1985).

Something to do

> *The youth club must give them opportunities to do something, rather than be about stopping them doing things.*
>
> (Youth Clubs UK, 1999)

The activities provided in clubs, should be many and varied (see Chapter 4). Having a variety of activity sessions in youth clubs will help young people develop new skills and enthusiasms. Some of these, such as canoeing or rock climbing, may normally be inaccessible to them, and the opportunity to try a new and exciting activity such as motor bike scrambling, gliding, skiing or sailing is something that many young people will seize. It is often possible for youth clubs to keep the cost of these activities low, by obtaining funding from charities etc. In the 1980s, projects working with young unemployed people could often fund residential experiences including outdoor activities. The acquisition of a new skill is valuable at any age, but particularly so for young people who may feel they are failures at school. Some clubs have been able to develop exciting initiatives which not only develop young people's skills, but also enable them to be more involved in the community. For example, at Lydney Youth Club in the Forest of Dean, a circus skills project (*The Guardian*,

6.3.2002), led to a show produced by young people, which toured local schools and raised issues about bullying.

Many young people are attracted to risk, and many end up getting into trouble because of it. Exciting activities can help provide an equivalent 'buzz', as a young man said to me about a blindfold trail in which he took part. Boys interviewed for the Listen Up Report (*The Guardian*, 11.4.2000), made a plea for more opportunities to take part in dangerous activities in safe settings.

The Duke of Edinburgh Award, and other youth awards schemes, can give a focus to developing skills. Many youth clubs are involved in delivering these schemes and young people can gain a tremendous amount. As one young person said:

> *It's made me more persistent, made me push myself harder. I have to organise things for myself and I'm more independent as a result.*
>
> (Stannard, 2000)

Someone to talk to

In Williamson's research (1995), young people identified other people to talk to as particularly important for advice and understanding, 'someone who could be trusted.'

Young people don't necessarily want hard facts or answers, and if they do there are better places to get them than the youth club, but youth workers can be a channel for accessing more specialist advice. As Taylor (2003) says, while some young people need specialist help and counselling most need only friendly support from adults. Youth clubs provide an ideal venue for these informal meetings. Young people may need to discuss the pressures of adolescence – many feel constantly harassed and stereotyped as trouble-makers, simply because of their age. 'Stressed' is a word they use to describe it. Important feedback from an evaluation of the Youth Action Scheme I managed in Gloucestershire, was the phrase from young people about the youth workers 'They treated us like adults, they showed us respect'. The important ingredient of youth work is the development of trusting relationships in a framework of confidentiality. In the Children and Young People's Unit consultation, after 'places to go' the next priority for young people was to be listened to, thus, 'I would change the way adults treat us, as if we are nothing but little kids without options' (www.cypu.gov.uk).

Several young people interviewed by the Institute for Public Policy Research felt the lack of someone older who they could turn to in times of trouble or talk to about the big issues in their lives (Edwards and Hatch, 2003). Young people positively rated the existence of rapport between them and youth workers (Bradford, 2004).

Space of our own

Teenagers feel stressed not only by the pace of life today but also because their parents and families do not provide the peer group environment that adolescents need (Coward, 2001). Maybe this explains the fascination with the boarding school world of Harry Potter, but more attention needs to be paid to the needs of young people growing up today. Children's freedoms have been curtailed by over-vigilant parents protecting their children from strangers, by schools forcing them to be tested constantly and overburdening them with homework, but also by their environment, with the danger from cars, and a lack of public transport. Children need space in which to relate freely to their peer group and to their community. Another worrying trend recently has been what Birkett (2001) describes as 'the privatization of parenthood'. With the potential introduction of curfews, she felt that the community responsibility for raising children was being lost. Children are being kept in, so they don't bother other adults, kept in to do what most people suggest they do too much of – computer games and watching television. What young people need is somewhere outside the home to go to meet their friends, which a youth club provides. Young people hanging around are often perceived as a problem by adults, but this may be the 'only autonomous space that young people are able to carve out for themselves' (Valentine et al., 1998, quoted in Brent, 2000).

It is very difficult for many young people to move around freely. The argument about the need for space for young people can be made without having to argue the educational benefits of youth work, as Williamson (1997) suggests:

> *There is a case for constructing youth work not on the high-faluting educational agenda, which continues to hold the theoretical high ground at present, but on a more modest social agenda which argues that teenagers have a right to social space.*

This is not a new idea. It was felt that the new Albermarle buildings 'must provide a place where friends can meet, talk and enjoy each others company, and where they can feel that they are in a place of their own' (Ministry of Education, 1962).

Recently the Impact of Youth Work survey (DfES, 2005: 151) showed that 'what brings young people into the youth service are the traditional things it has always offered – a place to go, people to meet, the youth workers, the activities, and the opportunity to make decisions about what they do'.

Since I have been in youth work, this argument has not been seen as valid by many youth service providers; it has had to be 'dressed up' in the educational language of learning outcomes. However, growth and development are mainly achieved through the part we play in the lives of others and they in ours.

Peer groups

Popular theories on adolescence agree that it is a time when peer group influence is of crucial importance. Acceptance of peer culture is complementary to parental authority and is an important step on the brink of adolescence, expanding social horizons, helping personality development and helping to develop the ability to act independently and try out new roles (Cotterell, 1996). Adolescence is a peak time of leisure needs and of time for leisure activities, but adolescents are restricted by lack of money and transport, and by parental and legal boundaries. Youth clubs can provide a safe environment from which to observe and interact with peers and to experience the roles of leader and follower. Psychologically, adolescence may be regarded as a period when individuals resolve the two key emotional processes, attachment and identity. Cotterell (1996) suggests that group identity comes first. Young people need to resolve their group identity and relationship to their peer group before they can achieve a sense of personal identity or resolve relations with their family. Peer friendships are at the core of healthy social growth and many young people, who are at odds with their peers, will have difficulties in many other aspects of life. The youth club provides an after-school arena to test out and make new friendships, and skilled youth workers can use group work techniques, such as those illustrated by Button (1974; 1981), to help young people with this core skill.

Interactions provide social conditions which create community, confirm identity and prevent loneliness. Over time, they embed people into a community. Youth clubs can be one way of ensuring that these interactions occur. The role of the youth worker is to facilitate conversations and provide space for them, but is also to be a 'social architect' (Button, 1974), helping young people to come together and work in groups.

Exclusion from public space

Youth clubs and centres are now more necessary as young people are excluded from what were once public spaces (shopping centres, etc.) and conflicts increase between young people and adults in public spaces. An argument against building-based work is that it segregates young people from the rest of society – but they are already segregated.

Brent (2001) writes about the way that the problems of a community are often seen by adults as stemming from young people, and the young people can be seen by adults as holding the area back from becoming a community.

Brent describes how young people develop their own places to go, but instead of adults welcoming the sight of teenagers organising their own activities (his example is the use of a woodland area for motor biking) – they stop them using it.

Many writers have argued for the need for public space for young people, and a powerful argument has been put by Sennett (1977), that the decline in public space has left us unable to deal with public issues without experiencing them as personal ones. The youth club can fill the need for a space for different types of people to meet and take risks with comparative strangers.

Keeping them off the streets

An argument for youth clubs which is more commonly used than the need for a space of their own is that young people need 'keeping off the streets'. As Mary Blandy points out in her inimitable story of a youth club, *Razor Edge* (1967) this idea is fundamental to youth work. I would argue that we should not be ashamed of trying to do this. Certainly young people often describe the youth club as 'keeping us off the streets' (Robertson, 2001) which they feel is a positive benefit, as the streets are a risky place to be. Bradford (2004) found that the youth club was regarded as a safe space to meet friends and enjoy themselves, they felt it also kept them away from crime and drugs. The top four reasons for going to the club were: friends go, a good place, good activities and nothing else to do.

Increasingly, youth services have been putting money into detached projects, which meet young people on their own territory. Apart from being cheaper to fund, these projects are often short term. In fact only 26 per cent of Detached Youth Workers are on more than three year contracts, and 46 per cent are on less than two year contracts (Rapport, March 2003), which does not allow the time to build up long term relationships with young people (see Chapter 3). Many detached projects see their role as providing information and advice to young people and workers are 'equipped' with leaflets. Workers certainly need to use their skills of engaging in conversation to maintain relationships in what are often very difficult circumstances. The combination, of detached workers and a well-run and equipped centre in an area, can engage a large proportion of young people.

Theoretical perspectives

In this section I discuss briefly some theoretical perspectives that can be used to argue the case for youth clubs.

Socialisation

As young people grow up, the various adults with whom young people interact are important as role models and to help young people fit into their adult roles. This is known as socialisation, 'the process whereby individuals in a society absorb the values, standards and belief current in that society' (Coleman and Warren-Adamson, 1992). Everyone in a society learns through the agents of socialisation such as the school, home, mass media and youth organisations. Youth workers can fill an important role for young people attending youth clubs by acting as an influential adult with whom they can develop an adult relationship that is different from those that they form with their parents or teachers. As a youth club leader wrote in 1933:

> *To get to know and to understand really well every individual member he must have it felt that he is their friend and their servant.*
>
> (Henriques, 1933: 61)

Transitions

Sociologists often define youth as a series of transitions from childhood dependency to adult citizenship. These transitions were traditionally regarded as being from full-time education to employment, from family of origin to family of destination, from residence with parents to living away from home. These are also known as school to work, domestic and housing transitions. During the last 20 years, research has shown that these transitions are becoming extended, i.e. are taking place at a much later age, as more young people are unemployed or in full-time education after 16. Also Coles (1995) suggests that many young people experience 'fractured' transitions, i.e. leave education without obtaining employment or leave home with nowhere to live, and that particular groups are most at risk, e.g. young people leaving care. There is particular concern about a group of young people aged between 16 and 18 for whom the term 'status zero' was coined (Williamson, 1997) – these young people are also described as NEET (Not in Education, Employment or Training). The Connexions Service (DfEE, 2000; Chapter 2) was set up to work with these young people, many of whom are involved in youth clubs, and youth clubs are increasingly used as bases for Connexions personal advisors to contact young people during 'drop in' sessions.

The focal theory of leisure

Coleman's original 'focal theory' of adolescent development (Coleman and Hendry, 1990) argued that the transition between child and adult could not be achieved without substantial adjustments, both psychological and social.

They suggest that concern about relationships with the opposite sex declines from a peak around 13 years old, concerns about peer acceptance and rejection are crucial at 15, while issues about independence from parents peak beyond mid-adolescence and then begin to tail off. In tandem with this, Hendry proposed a focal theory of leisure (Hendry et al., 1993). This suggests a different and changing pattern of leisure focus, from clubs organised by adults to casual leisure pursuits, to commercially organised leisure. The transitions between these are at the ages where the main relationship issues come into focus, first gender and self-identity, then peer relationships, then conflict with parents. This pattern was highlighted by research into youth work with vulnerable young people (Furlong et al., 1998). The young people in this study reported spending a significant proportion of their time 'hanging around'. In this middle phase, around age 15, young people are looking to run things themselves and need 'just enough' organisation, which a good youth club can provide. Youth organisations which try to be too bossy or controlling will not retain young people as they get older, or attract those young people whom Williamson (1997) describes as 'at the sharp end' and whose lives are chaotic.

Social networks

The concept of social networks shows the importance of social ties; friendships are embedded in a broader system through the social ties of each friend with others, giving access to new people. Adolescence is a period when growth in social networks, what we might call the development of social capital (see Chapter 8 and Field, 2003), is needed to develop competencies for adult life. Therefore, young people need opportunities for widening social networks, and out-of-school activities are important, giving access to young people of different ages and backgrounds. Obviously accessibility is important for network growth, for opportunities to make new friendships and build on existing ones. Work I did within the youth service, on removing barriers to participation by disabled young people, highlighted the social isolation they can suffer by attending special schools and by not mixing with young people in their communities.

Through attending a youth club, young people build up a personal network of supportive ties. Some members of the network are needed to help bridge changing settings or circumstances – this could be a role for a youth worker.

Complexity theory (Cillers, 1998) also points to the idea that making connections is important for human beings, and Gilchrist's (1999; 2004) work shows the importance of networks, both for personal growth and development and for community growth. The premise that young people who learn the skills of participation early in life will be better able to transform their communities as adults is another good reason for being serious about community provision for young people.

Norwegian research showed that young people who generally met their friends in organised settings had 30 per cent more adults and 50 per cent more peers as members of their networks than those who met friends on street corners or elsewhere (Cotterell, 1996). Talking about the area where he works in Bristol, Brent (2002) argues that there are 'insiders' and 'outsiders' – often local people will complain about people from outside coming to find out 'what is wrong with' them. Sennett (1977) challenged the whole idea that local communities are necessarily good things, leading as they do to the 'us and them scenario'. To counter this territorialism one of the experiences youth clubs can arrange is that of meeting people outside the immediate area e.g. inter-club visits and area events which can help young people build wider networks.

Political education

Political education was a much discussed concept in youth work in the 1970s and 1980s. Bunt and Gargrave explored this theme extensively in *The Politics of Youth Clubs* (1980). They felt that youth clubs should have much more governance by members.

Nowadays there is national concern about the decline in numbers voting at elections, particularly of young people. Youth clubs can give young people the opportunity to experience being involved in the democratic process in a small but meaningful way. Young people can become involved in their local club and on its management committee and, through the club, in local youth forums and parliaments.

The youth club provides an ideal environment for debating ideas and issues, drawing together young people and adults with different experiences and beliefs (Hollin, 1987). For many young people, the youth club may be the only place where their ideas and beliefs are taken seriously, and they are listened to. They will also have their ideas challenged and learn from each other and from staff.

Certainly politics should not be something that youth workers are afraid of. Youth people need a political understanding and they get so much propaganda from the right wing press and media that an alternative view doesn't really stand much chance, but it may sow a seed. Traditionally youth work has used the 'political with a small p argument', that political education isn't about party politics. However, the decisions that youth workers make, and their political or ethical stance, have repercussions for their work with young people (Banks, 1993). How workers use their power and authority in the club is a model for young people.

Citizenship and democracy

The government is currently concerned about the making of 'good citizens' – Brew was also saying this in 1943. The making of good citizens can only be done in a society where each member is important and is given a chance to contribute to the life of the group. This is difficult to apply in a large bureaucratic organisation such as a school, but a youth club provides an ideal environment for young people to exercise responsibility and learn to be accountable to their peers for the decisions they make. Most youth clubs have elected management committees in which young people are involved, plus members committees consisting entirely of young people.

Social education

This term was the defining term for youth work for much of its history (Davies and Gibson, 1967; Booton, 1985; Smith, 1988; Marsland, 1993). The Albermarle Report (Ministry of Education, 1960) asserted that the Youth Service provided for 'continued social and informal education of young people in terms most likely to bring them to maturity, that of responsible personal choice'. Davies and Gibson (1967) saw social education as a process, undertaken by youth workers and directed at the social development of adolescents. They felt young people needed to be offered a wide range of activities and pursuits so that they could develop through experiences.

Marsland (1993) saw youth work as complementary to schools, a preparation for life that schools could not provide, but that young people needed to acquire moral values. The needs of young people in his view can't be met without adult support, which facilitates the growth of 'mature autonomy' in young people. In *Developing Youth Work* (1988, www.infoed.uk) Smith provides an extensive critique of the concept, and he feels its individualistic orientation is now even more prevalent in recent initiatives such as *Transforming Youth Work* (DfEE, 2001) see Chapter 8.

Informal education

A club is a community engaged in the task of educating itself.

(Brew, 1943)

The best description of what informal education means for youth and community workers and how to go about it, is in Jeffs and Smith's handy guide '*Informal Education*' (1999) where they define informal education as 'the process of fostering learning in life as it is lived'. Informal educators are teachers in that they foster environments for learning. The role of a club worker is more similar in some ways to a teacher in a formal setting than to a detached youth worker, in that you do have some control over the environment. This depends, of course, on whether the youth club has its own premises or is using the village hall. However, wherever you are, some things can be changed about the environment to make it conducive to engaging in informal education. As Dewey stressed (www.infed.org), we can work with chance environments or design them for the purpose, and youth clubs should be designed for the purpose of informal education. By the environment is meant not only the physical setting but what activities are going on in it. As conversation is central to the work of an informal educator, it follows that we should be concerned to create spaces for conversation, and for small group work, as much as for ball games. Unfortunately, although many of the Albermarle purpose-built buildings did incorporate small spaces for this purpose, lack of staff has often meant their use being restricted and used for occasional meetings or even as offices. Conversations, however, can happen anywhere and it is up to the youth worker to be looking for opportunities and creating them. Too often a worker will spend quite a period of time with a group of young people, perhaps playing pool or in the minibus, without engaging them in conversation. The culture of the club, and whether conversation is expected and encouraged is important too. In some clubs young people are not expecting anyone to ask them about themselves or to want to talk to them. There was quite a persistent rumour in one club in which I did some research, that I was a policeperson, as I spent time asking the young people about the club and themselves, and they were not accustomed to being asked questions! It is the job of a youth worker to know about the young people they work with, names, where they go to school, who they hang around with, what they like doing etc. One of the performance indicators for centre based work must be that staff can tell you about the young people, and vice versa.

Heath and McLaughlin's research in the USA (1993) showed how young people learn from everyday settings. They focused on the daily life of organisations judged effective by local young people who felt they had no place in school and wanted something to do to get off the streets. They showed the development of young people through socio-cultural activities such as making biscuits to sell. They demonstrate how youth organisations can offer experiences to young people of learning together and working to shared goals.

Developmental needs of young people

The developmental needs of young people, which Button (1974) defines as 'the need for security, the need for new experiences, the need for significance, for relationships with peers, the need for responsibility and coming to terms with authority and for a coherent world view' can all be met within a youth club setting. Social experiences are crucial for young people. Button (1974) suggests that the peer relationship is one of the hardest for young people to establish. He did research in youth clubs to see how developmental group work methods could be made to work in a youth club setting (Button, 1975). He found that it was certainly possible to work effectively with small groups by assigning and training staff to work in this way. However, one of the major problems about doing this type of work is the high level of staffing needed to allow workers to work with small groups, and also the good management, supervision and support that workers need (see Chapter 6).

The recent research done into the impact of youth work by DeMontfort University found that two thirds of the young people in their survey (DfES, 2005) said that youth work had made a considerable difference to their lives, including confidence, making new friends, learning new skills, making decisions for themselves and feeling more able to ask for help and information when needed.

Chapter 2

The Roller Coaster History of Youth Clubs

Everything is as it is because everything was as it was.

(Saffran Foer, 2003)

The history of youth clubs can be described as a roller coaster ride, starting off on a steep ascent during the last half of the 19th century and continuing more slowly uphill until after the Second World War. After that there were spending cuts around 1948 and a descent downhill. In the early 1960s the government's adoption of the Albermarle Report (Ministry of Education, 1960) took the roller coaster up to new heights, but it did not stay there and began a slow descent in the1970s, which accelerated during the Thatcher years, until it seemed to be heading into and under the ground. In fact, while youth clubs are still in some ways underground, the youth service roller coaster has changed track onto Connexions and Youth Development which may still give it an exciting and uncertain ride. Youth clubs seem to be still waiting for a new roller coaster to take them back up again. Perhaps new initiatives such as 'Making Space' and '51 Minutes' (see below and Chapter 8) may provide such an impetus or the advent of Children's Trusts may see only those clubs in the voluntary sector survive.

This chapter looks at the history of clubs and ends with recent developments. Inevitably I also look more generally at the history of the youth service and, because I believe in the importance of understanding our history, I also refer to historical developments in other chapters. As Davies (1999) explains, the issues and concerns that we debate have deep roots in the past of the service and some historical understanding can help youth workers validate their practice instead of being left groping for arguments (Booton, 1985).

Beginnings

Youth clubs have a rich heritage. They developed in the United Kingdom over the last century and a half, from about the 1860s. These early clubs were usually single sex and were set up by Victorian middle class philanthropists, primarily for the purpose of 'improvement' (Booton, 1985: 9). Britain was one of the earliest countries to experience the range of social problems arising from the industrial revolution. The squalor of Victorian poverty and the cruel conditions under which children worked have been well documented by writers such as Dickens. The new industrial society approached the issue of young people in three ways, by providing schooling, by regulation of employment and by providing leisure activities. This aspect was developed by voluntary and philanthropic agencies, mainly from religious backgrounds (Leighton, 1972). These pioneers of youth work were grappling with enormous social problems.

Early accounts

There have been several accounts of this early period which illuminate the world of the clubs.

In his 1953 book Eager produced a History of Boys Clubs and Related Movements in Great Britain and this impressive volume makes interesting reading today. He includes some wonderful images of early provision and demonstrates how the various strands of provision came together in the idea of clubs. Eager (1953) traces their history though the Ragged Schools movement, Sunday Schools and Working Men's institutes, he describes the origin of the term 'Club', before it acquired its social welfare connotation. Up to the middle of the 19th century, clubs were places for social enjoyment for men, conspiratorial groups such as the Jacobin clubs or organisations for a special activity. In Victorian Britain London was full of gentlemen's clubs and they were much described in the literature of the period.

'Robertson of Brighton' 1816–1853, formed the Brighton Working Men's Institute in 1849 – for recreation and cultural education. Robertson argued that the 'intelligence of working men, many of whom were Chartists, should be given outlet and expression, if it were baulked their energies and ambitions would be diverted to social agitation and hostility to religion' (quoted in Eager, 1953).

The masculine ethos associated with clubs even today can perhaps be traced to these origins.

The title 'Club' was first used in 1852 when the Colonnade Working Men's Club opened in Drury Lane to provide amusement and refreshment, newspapers and books. Henry Solly who wrote '*Working Mens Social Clubs and Educational Institutes*' (1867) was said to believe that 'heaven consists of working mens clubs' (Eager, 1953). Solly defined clubs as 'societies of working men formed to promote social intercourse, innocent amusement, mental improvement and mutual helpfulness embodying the conception of a brotherhood for the completest possible culture of its members as human beings – for their whole development as men – social fellowship, recreation and education in one organization'.

However, a falling off in membership began as young men joined and became 'a nuisance' to the older men. By 1859 the Colonnade Club had failed and opened its premises as the Colonnade Boys Home and Club. Youth institutes formed as clubs were 'swamped with boys' according to Solly.

Sweatman's *Youth Clubs and Institutes* (1863) is the earliest advocacy of specific youth provision (Booton, 1985).

The reason for the formation of the club in Sweatman's view was to provide recreation for youths:

> *It is the absence of any provision for their harmless recreation and the refusal to recognise their natural claim to it that has driven so many of them into bad ways.*

He described the institutes activities and religious purpose as 'aimed at member's happiness in an atmosphere of freedom, friendship, good manners and good humour'.

Bunt and Gargrave (1980) describe how the early pioneer youth workers who created boys and girls clubs were motivated by compassion for the young people, who were living in often appalling conditions in the big cities. They set out to alleviate conditions, and to compensate the young for the harshness of their lives.

The aim of the Sunderland Waifs Rescue Agency and Street Vendors club, as explored by Spence (2001) was to encourage the poor towards participation in respectable working class life, by providing an inviting alternative to the streets, and paternalistic guidance plus welfare benefits and temporary shelter. Rules were devised by a committee and included expulsion for gambling, swearing and smoking. The same types of rules are still applied in clubs today where large notices proclaim that 'anyone with drugs' will be immediately thrown out.

Working Lads Clubs by Charles Russell and Lilian Rigby was written in 1908. They felt that the majority of young people were animated only by a desire to have fun. Girls and boys came to the clubs straight from work and much of the early work of clubs, besides providing activities, sought to educate and inform, especially around issues concerned with work. Much of the early club work was carried out under the auspices of the settlement houses of which Toynbee Hall is probably the most famous example. The idea behind the first clubs was to prevent social ill from happening, rather than to bring about social change, and indeed one could argue that youth clubs have always been partly about containment, 'keeping them off the streets' and out of 'mischief' (see Chapters 3 and 7). Youth work became widespread with the mission movement of the 1870s and by 1885 clubs were established in all urban centres. In his (1889) book on boys clubs Tom Pelham charted the development of boys' club and institute work in London over a period of twenty years and found that the number of parochial institutes and clubs had expanded from under 20 to over 300 (www.infed.org.uk).

By 1900 girls clubs had begun to organise on a national basis and a recreational, educational basis had begun to replace the older welfare model of practice. The girls clubs were largely run by educated middle class women who were involved in reformist movements of the time. Booton's 1985 book incorporates Maud Stanley's *Clubs for Working Girls* (1890) which gives a wonderful picture of what the girls clubs were like. The curriculum attempted to raise the girls' awareness in order to improve their social skills:

> *A club for girls will do a great work, it will raise, enable, bring out the best traits in a girl, by it's wholesome pleasures, varied interests, human sympathies between ladies, and girls will make their lives happy and a good one.*

The club provided a place for working girls to find the recreation they needed after a day of more than 10 hours of hard industrial work. Stanley (1890) gives advice on how to start and manage a club and discipline and advise the girls in a very practical way. Booton (1985) feels that one of the central misconceptions about the history of youth work is that it began with clubs for boys, while in fact what he identifies as youth work i.e. 'self conscious systematic practice' began in the 1860s with the establishment of clubs for girls. This type of practice involving a conscious mode of intervention and a level of common understanding was developed later with boys, about 1910.

National organisation

By 1911 a National Association of Girls Clubs had been formed. A group of 18 women, convinced of the 'need for middle class leisured women to work to improve the lot of their working sisters' (Turnbull, 2001), formed a co-ordinating body with a focus on developing the industrial and recreational work undertaken by the clubs under one head. Women of very different persuasions were involved; from Victorian philanthropists to feminist organisations and the labour movement.

Motivation

Davies (1999) suggests that there were mixed motives behind the establishment of much early provision, which was targeted largely at 'factory girls and working class boys'. The idea of charity in the 1800s required that the giver mixed with the recipient to give something of their lifestyle and values. There are some wonderful examples of this type of charity in Dickens' writing, for example in Bleak House, where Mrs Pardiggle does her visiting rounds:

If I find a person unwilling to listen to what I have to say I tell that person directly, 'I am incapable of fatigue – I am never tired and I mean to go on until I am done'.

(Dickens, 1853)

By the later decades of the 19th century, much that was being done in the name of charity was being criticised as demoralising to the poor, so that the voluntary youth organisations pioneered an important new expression of the philanthropic spirit where the work bound the giver and the receiver closely together. Davies (1999) says this served to place relationships at the heart of youth work from the beginning. There were then religious and moral motives for youth club work, but also political concern about the masses and the threat of revolution. It was seen as essential that young people grew up fit and patriotic. Jingoism was part of the club's philosophy in some cases, with members joining up 'en masse' in the First World War.

State approval

Osgerby (1998) describes the rise of the youth service as a history of state intervention, deriving from concern about the behaviour of young people, in particular boys, who were seen as likely to become delinquent. Spence (2001) feels that the debate about delinquency stressed the preventative nature of club work, and that this view was then officially recognised. In 1916 the Home Office called the representatives of the voluntary sector, such as the Boys Brigade, together to form a Central Juvenile Organisations Committee. Its purpose was to liaise with educational bodies and co-ordinate the provision of recreational facilities for young people. These powers were then formalised by the 1918 and 1921 Education Acts, empowering local authorities to spend public money on youth facilities. Youth clubs at this time were not only in urban centres, they were also concentrated in industrial areas such as the Rhondda Valley in Wales where, for example, there were 52 clubs in the 1920s with a membership of 9,000 (Smith, 2001).

Although this did not lead to a great deal of expenditure by the state, it was an important step and paved the way for more intervention in 1937 with the Physical Training and Recreation Act due to concerns about the physical fitness of the young in the 1930s, with many policy makers convinced another war was inevitable. The first local authority youth centres came about when some authorities went beyond providing facilities for fitness, which they were empowered to pay for under the Act.

According to Booton (1985) the state was distrusted by many voluntary organisations as a threat to family responsibility and community self-help. He felt that the development of a statutory service became essential because of the failure of the voluntary organisations to reach the 'less accessible' young people, those now often described as 'disaffected.' In the 1930s, estimates of attachment to the voluntary youth organisations ranged from 15 to 30 per cent of the potential clientele, one in six in 1937 (Osgerby, 1998). By the 1940s and 1950s the 'unattached' were seen as a challenge to attract to provision (Davies, 1999).

The early working men's clubs had tended to become exclusive, taking on a bourgeois identity. Booton (1983) describes this as a familiar pattern, and it can be seen today where youth clubs end up excluding the very young people they are supposed to be working with. This phenomenon was experienced and described by Jimmy Boyle in his autobiography: 'Eventually the club lost its true purpose as it barred guys like me from coming in when in fact we should have been the ones to be stopped from leaving at any cost' (Boyle, 1977: 30).

Concerns about the fate of adolescents during the war, with fathers fighting and mothers working, and fears of a rise in juvenile crime (the number of under 17-year-olds convicted rose by over a third between 1939 and 1941) (Davies, 1999) led to feelings that 'something had to be done'. Circular 1486, *The Service of Youth* was issued in 1939. It accepted that youth organisations were an educational resource and acknowledged that there was a lack of facilities in many parts of the country. This was the first explicit identification by the government that youth work was an education service to be supported through local education authorities (Leigh and Smart, 1985; Smith, D., 1989). It made the Board of Education responsible for youth welfare and a branch of it was established to administer grants. Local youth committees were established locally and by 1940 some 1,700 new units had been set up (Davies, 1999). A later circular 1516, *The Challenge of Youth* focused more on philosophy and purpose, which it stated was the 'building of character'. This needed three elements: social facilities, physical recreation and continued education. It made it clear that the function of the state was to focus and lead efforts and to supplement the resources of the voluntary sector without compromising the independence of that sector.

The Welfare State

The post-war establishment of the Welfare State and the adoption of the Beveridge Report in 1942 led to increased state intervention and the youth service was included in this, with the 1944 Education Act establishing a role for the state within youth club work. However, state responsibility was still only to 'secure' facilities not to provide them directly (Sections 41 and 53), and it did not name a 'youth service.' It was designed to strengthen the role of local authorities but still leave them plenty of discretion (Davies, 1999).

Osgerby (1998) suggests that the post-war youth service was designed to function as a fully integrated component of the education system; there were even ideas that attending a youth club should be made compulsory! Maybe an idea that should be resurrected!

The problem was that there was no statement as to what adequate facilities might be (something the Youth Service has been plagued with ever since!), and this has led to great differences in provision throughout the country.

The youth service did grow, albeit irregularly, and by 1948 nearly 2,000 paid, full-time youth leaders were in post. Many of the new centres were directly run by the LEA, often in school buildings. However, continued backing by the State was not guaranteed and with spending cuts arriving in 1948 it seemed that the new service was already experiencing the first of many declines:

> *. . . local education authorities have made drastic cuts in youth service estimates to such an extent that the maintenance of essential facilities has been impaired.*
>
> (Resolution from the National Association of Youth Leaders and Organisers quoted in Davies, 1999: 27)

'The lean years' (Leighton, 1972)

School spending was prioritised, and lack of funding throughout the early 1950s left the youth service in a parlous state. Many commentators felt it was unlikely to survive (Davies, 1999; Jeffs, 1979). The numbers of training courses and people on them declined and very few LEAs had a coherent youth policy. There were no national standards and no accepted minimum provision.

However, by the end of the 1950s, with the children resulting from the post war baby boom growth in the population about to become adolescents, the growth of young people's spending power had become a concern (Davies, 1999; Osgerby; 1998). Working class young people had money to spend and there was more to spend it on. There were anxieties about 'mass culture' and the rise in juvenile delinquency. Too many young people were facing empty hours at the end of the day 'when their days work is finished – empty hours faced with empty heads, full pockets and high spirits' (BMA, 1961 quoted in Osgerby, 1998: 140) and they were not being catered for. Research, for example by Pearl Jephcott (quoted in Osgerby, 1988) suggested that youth clubs tended to draw their membership from the more respectable sections of the working and lower middle class rather than the 'below average 'child from the 'below average' home. Youth workers at the time felt neglected and held in small regard (nothing new there). A report from the King George Jubilee Trust felt that the 'service had been allowed to lose confidence when it should have been receiving encouragement, there were serious doubts as to whether it had a part to play in the lives of young people' (King George Jubilee Trust Citizens of Tomorrow, 1955; Davies, 1999). The riots of 1958 in Nottingham and Notting Hill, the 'rock and roll riots' when Bill Haley appeared, added to a growing 'moral panic' about young people, not helped by the prospect of the imminent end of National Service.

Davies (1999) suggests that there was an unusual combination of possibilities. An ideology favouring state intervention, changing social conditions and a more favourable economic climate that led to a House of Commons Select Committee focusing on the youth service for the first time; and thus to the Albermarle Report. There was also, as Holmes (1997) points out, an unprecedented level of lobbying and report writing by a wide range of people involved in the youth service in both the voluntary and statutory sector.

Albermarle

The reports' terms of reference were:

> *. . . to review the contribution which the Youth Service of England and Wales can make in assisting young people to play their part in the life of the community in the light of changing social and industrial conditions and of current trends in other branches of the education service: and to advise according to what priorities best value can be obtained for the money spent.*
>
> (Ministry of Education, 1960)

The committee consisted of people who could think creatively and also had political clout (Davies, 1999). Lady Albermarle herself, while an experienced committee person, was not a radical, but there were members who were determined to respond to the changes in young people's lives. These included Richard Hoggart, who contrasted the strengths of working class culture with the transience of the mass media, Leslie Paul, founder of the Woodcraft Folk, who brought his socialist and co-operative philosophy, and Pearl Jephcott with her experience in the National Associations.

The committee saw its function as 'to eliminate the frustration and sense of inferiority felt by unfortunate weaker brethren who get left behind at 15' to quote from a senior civil servant (Smith, 1997).

Albermarle's conclusions may seem to have been inevitable given the decline in the youth services but Davies (1999) stresses that it did recognise the distinctive approach of the youth service, especially the underlying principle of voluntary choice. Published in 1960, the report found the youth service to be in a critical condition, in particular the state of buildings used for youth work which were generally unfit for the purpose with drab, dreary and unheated rooms often in shared premises, and was immediately endorsed by the Ministry. Both main party manifestos of 1959 had included a commitment to improving the youth service (Holmes, 1997).The service went on to attract cross party support well into the 1970s.

Albermarle makes a critique of the 1950s which is fascinating reading today as it portrays the rise of a distinctive youth culture for the first time. The concept of a youth culture is familiar to us, and indeed has recently been challenged as a concept (Jeffs and Smith, 1998). However, at the time of Albermarle it was a new idea that young people had different interests and needs from adults.

The committee saw young people as 'affluent, iconoclastic and, culturally, highly distinctive'. Its proposals for the youth service aimed for it to free itself from its drab and ramshackle image and adopt a contemporary approach (Davies, 1999) with clubs providing a sophisticated modern setting. It was a universalist approach, to offer the service to all young people, but with a priority given to young working class people. There was a very positive approach to youth work and its ability to release young people's potential. Social education was stressed throughout and the youth service's activity programme was said to offer three kinds of experience; association, training and challenge.

Evans (1965) suggest that there was a changed emphasis in club work following Albemarle, the function of a mixed club was now seen as a social one. The main object being to provide a meeting place where interests and activities could arise spontaneously from the life of the group. Previously the emphasis had been on creating a community with standards and loyalties and traditions which were accepted by and followed by their members.

'The Golden Age'

> *If the youth service ever had a golden age then the 1960s was certainly it.*
>
> (Davies, 1999)

There was steady expansion of youth club provision over the decade. By 1964 local education authorities had more than doubled their youth service budgets. The number of full-time workers more than doubled in the following ten years, half of them trained at a new National College (Smith, 1997).

Albermarle had promised 'bright and gay' buildings, an imaginative building programme commenced, and £28 million was spent on three thousand building projects (Smith, 1997). Two Youth Service Building Bulletins were issued by the Ministry of Education, No. 20 September 1961 on General Mixed Clubs and No. 22, Withywood Bristol in 1963. It was felt that the general mixed club was most likely to be the type in demand. It aimed to give young people who had left school an equivalent setting to

Figure 2.1 Withywood: the central space

those who had gone to university, and were part of students' unions. However, only a cursory look today in Bristol will show what actually happened. Withywood is now a run-down shadow of its former self, while the students' unions are major providers of recreational and leisure facilities.

There were some imaginative designs for the new buildings, but some of the most interesting ideas were perhaps never really practical, demanding a high level of staff and resources. For instance, Withywood had a central space with a removable floor. The floor was sunk one foot below the normal level and filled by linoleum-topped platform units which provided a flat surface over the whole of the ground floor on normal evenings. When these units were removed they revealed a hardwood block floor suitable for dancing and the units could be used for seating in various ways so that the space could be used for drama or film shows or even a table tennis match or fashion parade. There were also spiral stair cases leading up to a large balcony area. Both of these features have now gone – a sad loss of our heritage.

The general principles of these new buildings were outlined in the Ministry Bulletin No. 20 (1961). They included several questions which needed to be answered before an architect could be briefed, about numbers expected to attend, age range, range of facilities and the clubs place and function in the youth service development scheme for the area:

> *The general club should operate on the broadest possible front offering its members the widest practical variety of facilities and experience. The first and most important function is socialisation; it must provide a place where friends can meet, talk and enjoy each others company, and where they can feel that they are in a place of their own.*

They were aiming for a sophisticated physical environment to attract young people who had not used it before. They usually offered areas for physical sporting activity, quiet rooms, a dance area and craft rooms equipped with work benches and sinks. However, by 1976 a report undertaken by Eggleston found that the majority of active members were aged 14–16, less mature than those for whom the buildings were designed, and they needed areas in which to 'let off steam'.

Training

One important recommendation of the Albermarle Report was the increase in training courses to produce the new workers required to staff the buildings. The National College opened in 1961 at Leicester. Part- time staff training was also given an impetus by the Bessy Report of 1962 which advised on part-time and volunteer training.

The voluntary sector

While voluntary sector clubs and organisations still played a large part in the national youth service provision Albermarle established the role of the State as a major provider of youth work provision, and local authorities as having an overall responsibility in their area.

After Albermarle

Throughout the 1960s across the country buildings similar to Withywood were constructed, all usually with open plan social areas designed to be used simultaneously for many different activities. Davies (1999) suggests that, although initially thought successful, the Withywood model was perhaps a product of unrealistic diagnosis of need and function plus rock-bottom initial costings. Also, budgets were not large enough to cope with the repair demands. By 1967, fuller use of capital resources by the community was being urged, and there was a reduction in the youth service building programme designed to improve value for money, by having multi-use buildings.

Although the Albermarle report had an incredible impact on the history of youth clubs, and indeed its legacy is still around us in every town where an Albermarle building was built, its philosophy was undermined by later reports and by cuts in public spending. Its ambitious building plan which led to 'glass palaces' did not lead to enough outlay locally in revenue to maintain the buildings properly, or to staff them for the facilities they provided. It was no good having an arts room if there was no one to staff it, and gradually areas began to be used for store rooms, or rented out to local groups such as the playgroup, thus making them unavailable for young people. These buildings were not always practical for the needs of young people, large halls are ideal for ball games but not where the walls are largely glass, and breakable. It was often difficult to persuade the local authority to install toughened glass, being more expensive and somehow coming from a different budget than the emergency repair of broken glass. That was my experience anyway! Withywoods wonderful design features such as the moveable wood block floor and spiral staircase were removed on health and safety grounds in the 1990s.

Apart from a lack of funding there was also still debate about the direction of the service. Figures suggested there was an increase in attendance throughout the 1960s, but this was open to doubt (Davies, 1999) particularly as the number of young people in the population was rising. In 1965 it was acknowledged that clubs were still not attracting 'the unattached'. Projects were developed to target the 'alienation' of young people (Davies, 1999).

The 1970s Milson–Fairburn, the arrival of community work

Lack of direction in a colder climate.

(Thompson et al., 1982)

The Youth Service Development Council was brought into existence by the Albermarle report. Acting as a national pressure group, it consisted of many influential practitioners and academics in the field of youth work. Two sub-committees were formed, one to look at the relationship of the service with schools and further education, chaired by Andrew Fairburn, and one to look at the relationship with 'the adult community', chaired by Fred Milson (DES, 1969). The Minister, Denis Howell, wanted the committees to take a fundamental look at the service, particularly the different needs of different age groups.

The report, *Youth and Community Work in the 1970s* was issued in 1969. It used the concept of communitarianism, drawing on the work of Etzioni, the American sociologist. His idea of the 'active society' also influenced Tony Blair 25 years later. No clear direction for the service emerged, perhaps due to the different departure points and ideologies of the two committees (Davies, 1999). Fairburn advocated more integration of youth work and schools whilst

Milson wanted to move youth work facilities away from buildings and membership and saw the school as part of the community rather than its focus. Politically the report was seen as left-leaning (Marsland, 1993; Davies, 1999). The Labour government fell the following year, before any action had been taken on the report. In May 1970 Margaret Thatcher became Minister of Education and, in a less well publicised decision than that of the 'milk snatching' policy, she rejected the report, affirming that the emphasis should continue to be on youth work. She also decreed that more resources should be targeted on deprived areas. Davies (1999) feels that this is the first example of the state explicitly making targeting a priority for the youth service and a move away from generic club provision. At grass roots level the advent of Milson–Fairbairn, despite any national initiative, led to much linking of 'community' with 'youth' in organisational titles (Davies, 1999). Marsland (1993) felt that the effect of Milson–Fairbairn was 'to propagate confusion and threaten distraction from the proper objectives of youth work' which he saw as the social education of young people. He felt that in practice it led to the running down of clubs and the allocation of resources to detached work and that 'the youth service should not be distracted from their real, essential and immensely valuable work by the tempting sirens of 'community'. Different sirens exist today to lure youth work managers, offering short-term funding for many different projects.

Cuts

During the 1970s, and despite the election of a Labour government in 1974, there was no coherent policy on the youth service and it was subjected to the cuts experienced by all public services, but often to a greater degree because of the lack of a national statutory service with clear standards. Attempts were made to remedy this with private members bills being introduced with cross party support, in 1974, 1975 and again in 1979, which required that LEAs co-ordinate youth provision. However, in the early 1970s it seems that overall expenditure did increase on the local authority youth service (Davies, 1999) and it was only really with the advent of the Thatcher government in 1979 that cuts in real terms were experienced. The voluntary sector was increasingly threatened as responsibility for capital grants was given to LEAs and then withdrawn, while the traditional voluntary sector experienced funding difficulties and was encouraged to look elsewhere for funds. An independent sector working with some of the most deprived young people, such as the young homeless, began to develop on the back of short term funding strategies, such as Urban Aid.

Liberation movements

The liberation movements and ideas of the 1970s impacted on the youth service (see Chapter 5), alerted workers to the demands of oppressed groups, and also made them examine their own attitudes, leading to the rise of issue-based work in the 1980s. Other influences on youth work in the 1970s were theoretical, with group work methods and ideas such as those of Klein (1956), Button (1971 and 1974) and Milson (1973) used in the training of youth workers. Counselling was also more widely discussed and Bunt and Gargrave (1980) felt there was a shift from a social/recreational approach towards a welfare/pathology approach to the work, and a change in the role of adults from 'custodial and paternalistic to stimulator and creator of community opportunities'.

Meanwhile, youth clubs were still working with young people and in 1975 a survey showed that organisations like the National Association of Boys Clubs and NAYC were attracting mainly 14 to 18-year-olds, with more working class members than the uniformed organisations, who catered mainly for 10 to 14-year-olds (Davies, 1999).

The 1980s: The Thompson Report

When I became a full-time worker in 1979 it seemed the morale of the service was at a low ebb. However, since then it is difficult to identify any high points (maybe youth workers are very difficult to please!) but little was done to please them during the 1970s and 1980s. Davies (1999) feels that staff were fearful for their long-term future and also distrustful of management, certainly there was no better way of getting worker solidarity than a good moan about the management.

A research project was set up by the DES, based at the National Youth Bureau, to look at training and the careers of those completing it. Reporting in 1981 it found that many qualified workers were not going into the traditional youth club service once qualified. Also those teacher trained workers in the youth service were not staying long and there was a split within the full-time workforce between building based, club workers and community work oriented workers (Holmes, 1981). Davies (1999) feels that centre-based work was left out of fashion and under-valued by these debates, it was portrayed as controlling of young people as opposed to radical and liberating.

This tension has been in the service for a long time and often shows itself when workers are gathered together, with detached workers feeling they are doing radical work at the sharp end, while building-based workers feel they do the really hard, but not so glamorous, graft. The tension between demand-led and issue-based work as described by Davies (1999) and in Chapter 7 is also still a real one in the service and is sometimes exemplified by workers claiming 'quality' rather than 'quantity' work for youth clubs: however quantity is vital or there will be no club atmosphere. Another important tension in the 1980s, which still exists today, was that between 'targeting' and 'generic provision'. These debates were bought to the fore by the Thompson Report, *Experience and Participation*, of 1982.

This came from a committee set up by the government, following the failed Youth Service private members bill of 1979. Looking back at the history of youth work the Thompson committee felt that the Albermarle Report had done an immense service to the youth movement, but 'conceptually it left behind it a host of loose ends which were to emerge rapidly as major problems in the following decade' (Thompson, 1982).

The report recognised the alienation of many young people, and the cracks in the structure of British society. Its survey of young people showed that they were concerned about unemployment, racism and homelessness. It asserted that the services 'sole objective' was the personal development of the individual and stressed the importance of social and political education in contrast with the recent DfES report (Merton et al., 2005) which identified social capital as the primary social and moral purpose of youth work. This means working with young people in groups and in communities. The report made gestures to participation and to work with young people at risk, with special needs, and from ethnic minorities. Weaknesses in current provision were identified as; lack of a theory of social education, patchy response to social needs and inadequate provision for over 16s, and were felt to be due mainly to poor management and to poor training of workers. It wanted to see a stronger legislative base for the service, but not defined standards for local provision. Thompson (1982) estimated that some two thirds of 14 to 19-year-olds had attended a youth club at some time but only about 3 in 10 did so regularly, and the majority of those were under 16. This, combined with financial pressures, led to an increase in detached work, most of which was focused on so called 'problem' young people involved in illegal drug use and other crime (Davies, 1999). There was also a growth in specialist counselling services for young people, and information shops. Thompson (1982) also felt the service should be providing for the unemployed, and noted that they were more likely to use youth clubs than the employed – hardly surprising given the lack of funds of the unemployed! Clubs tended to make space and workers available to unemployed young people and many local authorities provided funding for activities and residential experiences.

The government refused to legislate on the recommendations of Thompson, but the report had some impact on the ground with many local authorities reorganising their services (Davies, 1999) and many at least *attempted* to promote work with young people with disabilities and young black people.

Youth unemployment

Young people's deprivation became a real issue with the rise in unemployment among the young, rising from 3 per cent of 16-year-olds in 1974 to 11 per cent in 1979, by 1984 it was 26 per cent including those on government schemes. Griffen (1993) suggests that it was the threat of unstructured free time of young people, due to unemployment, that led to the government and local authority initiatives throughout the 1980s, including funding for youth centres to open their doors to unemployed young people. Many youth club workers got involved in job creation projects like the Dundry Slopes Project in Withywood (Acta, 2002). The main government response was through the Manpower Services Commission, which became 'the biggest local employer north of Watford' (Davies, 1999). As targeting became a policy imperative, the numbers of 'unattached' young people grew. A study of youth service take-up concluded that overall attendance was around 26 per cent of young people, and concerns about delinquency also grew. The Intermediate Treatment Initiative (for diversionary work with young people) was set up following the 1969 Children and Young Persons Bill. Youth services, however, did not really get involved to any extent (Davies, 1999).

More cuts

Throughout the 1980s, cuts continued in youth service budgets as part of the overall cuts on public spending imposed by the Conservative Government. The only new money appearing during this time was from short-term funding initiatives, such as the Home Office's Section 11, targeted at work with ethnic minority groups. An important impact on the service was also the abolition of the large metropolitan councils, the Greater London Council (GLC) and the Inner London Education Authority (ILEA). This particularly affected funding for voluntary groups.

The Manpower Services Commission (MSC) administered Youth Training Scheme (YTS) and Community Programme had an impact on the service as, despite trade union opposition, many youth workers became involved in delivering life skills training to YTS trainees and running community programmes. Even with no active involvement from the youth workers, many youth club buildings became host to community programme initiatives such as after-school clubs or cafes. To some commentators this showed the youth service's willingness to compromise its principles and dance to the governments tune, to others like Marsland (1993) 'the oppositional stand of some youth workers led to lack of confidence in the service from government'. The same arguments can be seen in the present debate over Connexions and Transforming Youth Work.

National Advisory Council

Following Thompson, a National Advisory Council for the Youth Service (NACYS) was set up in 1985. It was intended to look at the most effective deployment of youth service resources – targeting was still on the agenda (Davies, 1999). It produced reports on youth work in rural areas, girls work and work with disabled young people. A consultation paper *Directions for the Youth Service* concluded that there was still a need for 'the mainstream range of provision for the average young person who wants somewhere to go, to be with friends, to pursue interests, to be offered new experiences, to talk over feelings' (NACYS, 1989) i.e. youth clubs. However, it felt that the service should move to more targeted forms of provision, and that priority should be given to those who were least likely to have access to personal and social development experiences. In a time of declining resources the service was unlikely to be able to do both. The report did press for greater autonomy for local youth clubs within their own communities and looked at raising standards of youth work, but the Council was disbanded by the government.

The 1990s

While nothing much may have changed in the day-to-day life of the youth club, the 1990s were a period of questioning and discussion about the future of youth work. Throughout the 1980s the youth service had moved more towards being a targeted rather than a generic service, with new government money only available for short-term funding, focused on areas of deprivation or particular groups of young people 'at risk' (Banks, 1993; Bradford, 1997). France and Wiles (1997) suggest that there is evidence that the funding base at local authority level was eroded, following on the trend in the 1970s and 1980s for youth services to be at the forefront of cost cutting exercises. Youth work proliferated in other areas such as health promotion and crime prevention and struggles continued to get the service to resource and acknowledge the need for separate provision for black groups, young women, young people with disabilities and young gay people.

The Youth Action Scheme

The Youth Action Scheme, which ran from 1993 to1996, was the largest example of a government funded short-term targeted scheme. Its main aim was to see if youth workers could reduce the risk of 'young people drifting into crime' (France and Wiles, 1997). Nearly £4 million was allocated by a bidding process. The prospect of so much money meant that local education authorities insisted that youth services put in bids, even where they were unwilling. Twenty-eight local authorities were awarded funds to run fifty-nine different projects, which eventually involved about 4,500 young people. However, despite the view of some police that 'there is a link between increased youth facilities and reduced levels of crime' (Davies, 1999) this new money did not go to actual provision of physical facilities for young people. The funding was not capital funding and had to be match funded by staffing or resources from the authority. Also, the provision was short term, so that projects were generally detached work projects operating in what were seen as 'high risk areas'.

The amount of money spent was large compared to most youth service budgets (Youth Service Audit, 1998) which aroused much resentment, particularly from centre-based youth workers who were seeing their budgets cut. Projects were under pressure to claim success to obtain continued funding for the succeeding years and detached work was promoted as a method of reaching young people with no clear idea of what impact, if any, it was having. France and Wiles (1997) considered that the youth service needed to learn lessons from their involvement in the Youth Action Scheme. They believed that youth workers needed to engage with the 'crime agenda', and demonstrate their ability to target those most at risk. In my view, however, as a manager of a Youth Action Scheme, another lesson which could have been learnt was that the youth service ought not to stray too far from its core business, i.e. clubs, and put too much reliance on short term funding.

A national curriculum?

The government established a national curriculum for schools and then started on the youth service. It had a three pronged attack as part of increasing managerial control; the establishment of a National Youth Agency, an attempt to get the service to agree a core curriculum and a review of the service (Davies, 1999). The National Youth Agency (NYA) was formed with the key functions of curriculum development, monitoring and evaluating of training. The idea of a curriculum had been around for a while, explicitly since 1975 when a National Youth Bureau (NYB) pamphlet asked 'What are we doing in this club?' under the title of *Curriculum Development in the Club*. There was, however, no clear idea of what a curriculum should look like, or even whether one was appropriate for youth work. Youth workers had always insisted that it was the way the work was done, rather than the content that was important, the process being more important than the task. Now the government wanted to take a close look at the content (Ord, 2004; Robertson, 2005) and articles in Youth Policy number 84.

Despite the NYA's involvement, or perhaps because of it, youth workers in the field were deeply suspicious. The frequent changes in government ministers that occurred throughout the process caused further problems with the initiative (Davies, 1999).

The curriculum conferences

The first of three curriculum conferences (NYB, 1990; Ord, 2004) involved Chief Education Officers and senior voluntary sector representatives. The government wanted to produce an agreement about the role of the service, including its target groups and what it should help them to achieve. There was extensive prior consultation with the field, but the process still seemed remote from fieldworkers, who were not invited to the actual conference. This was reflected by the conclusions of the conference, which were that more consultation was needed to achieve an agreed national statement.

More consultation nationally led to a statement of purpose for the second conference which did stress the 'importance of spontaneity' but there was also a focus on targets, outcomes and performance indicators. It may seem strange today but this was the first time youth workers had been asked to think about performance indicators, learning outcomes etc., at least in those terms. An imaginary extract from the diaries of Alan Howarth, the minister, in the *New Statesman* (Mugger, 1990) suggested that the conference was an outstanding success as, 'all the participants went home more confused and frustrated than when they arrived'. There were different understandings of the notion of 'curriculum', with the youth service considering it as 'process' and the DES and NYA seeing it as 'outcomes' (Davies, 1999).

The third conference followed regional and national consultation seminars and took place in June 1992. It laid plans for further work on performance indicators but, according to *The Times*, really meant 'no change' for the service (Davies, 1999). However, although there was much initial resistance to the idea of a curriculum the process initiated debates on 'the curriculum' across the country. This was a chance for workers to actually discuss the values of their work, and the statement of purpose was adopted by many services in broad terms, but with local differences. In these documents youth work is usually treated as a constant, however there were big differences between club work and targeted detached work in terms of practice and theory, which were never acknowledged.

Coopers and Lybrand Deloitte

Besides the conferences there was also a new review of the service carried out in 1990-91, by Coopers and Lybrand Deloitte, a private consultancy firm. Its remit was to examine how best the service could be managed in the context of the introduction of local management of schools. This aroused major suspicions within the service but in fact the consultants recognised the value of the voluntary relationships made with young people, and that it was difficult for the local authority youth service to have direct influence over the voluntary sector. It recommended a model 'for effective planning through partnership', involving performance indicators, business plans and the like. This language was in turn welcomed by many youth service managers (see Chapter 6). Davies (1999) feels that the report's effect was to reinforce a focus on management, rather than curriculum issues.

Performance indicators and monitoring statistics became prominent throughout the service. In 1994 the youth service inspectorate, Ofsted (DfE, 1994) issued a framework for inspecting youth services, emphasising the importance of value for money.

Take-up

Take-up of the service came into question after the survey Young People's Participation in the Youth Service (DfE, 1995) found that some two thirds of young people had been involved with the service at some time and 20 per cent of the 13 to 19 age group were currently involved. The figures (Davies, 1999) suggested that usage had dropped from about a third of young people over the previous 50 years to 20 per cent currently. This may have been partly to do with the fact that 25 per cent said they were put off by the poor facilities, many of which had seen no investment since their construction in the 1960s and a lack of staff to open premises. The Community and Youth Workers Union calculated that every authority was short of 50 full-time equivalent youth workers, following direct cuts in the 1980s and early 1990s.

Short-term funding

Available money was now more likely to come from short-term funding. Davies (1999) suggests that well before the lottery money was available in the late 1990s, the balance of youth service budgets was tipping away from mainstream, long-term funding to external and short-term funding. Jeffs and Smith (1999) suggest that this raises ethical issues for youth workers which have not always been fully thought through, issues of taking money from business sponsors for instance.

Youth clubs suffered from this shift as building-based work demands longer term finance. In fact many authorities were viewing 'detached' work as the answer to many of their financial problems. In the early 1990s the NYA was involved with several local youth services in looking at ways of managing the service including the possibility of contracting it out on a similar model to the careers service (Stead, 1992). Some services did contract out their services while others moved them to a community education structure or to leisure. Meanwhile local government reorganisation created new, smaller local authorities which were not always aware of the role of the youth service. A Sufficiency Working Group of the Community and Youth Workers Union (CYWU, 1994) attempted to establish the 'level of resourcing', 'the number of workers in an area', 'target groups' etc. Some services followed this up, but it was not taken up nationally. The discretion of local education authorities to spend money was becoming limited by schools opting out and by the spending demands of the national curriculum for schools. Attempts were made to get legislation on the youth service included in education legislation in the early 1990s including private members bills, but all fell.

More pressure was brought to bear politically by the formation in 1996 of a national youth work alliance which produced a pamphlet called *Agenda for a Generation* (NYA, 1996) proposing a set of minimum standards and a statutory basis for them. It concluded that youth work needed:

- An unequivocal statutory basis.
- Consistent public funding.
- A distinctive place in delivering national programmes.
- New machinery to co-ordinate national youth policies.
- Improved arrangements for quality assurance.
- A coherent framework of training and qualification.
- A vibrant national infrastructure.

New Labour

In the run up to the 1997 general election both the Labour and Liberal Democrat parties committed themselves to the introduction of a statutory youth service. The Labour party initiated a Youth Task Group, chaired by Peter Kilfoyle, a former youth worker, and its report favoured appointing a Minister for Youth and new legislation on the youth service. So, when Labour won a landslide victory in 1997, prospects for the youth service at last seemed to be coming good. However, the incoming government's policies on youth did not seem very progressive (Mizen, 2003) with the new minimum wage being set at a lower level for under 25-year-olds and with no reinstatement of benefit for 16 to 17-year-olds. Some of the government's first initiatives on youth were the establishment of youth offending teams and millennium volunteers,

The New Deal to get young people into work, and the establishment of Education Action Zones. Despite the fact that the amount of cash going to the youth service was shown to have fallen by 16 per cent in real terms since 1988 (Davies, 1999; Wylie, 2004) there was nothing for the youth service specifically. Labour did not publish its task force paper on youth issues and instead announced an audit of the service for the first time in its history. This consisted of a questionnaire to all local authorities and achieved a 100 per cent response. It showed a large variation in spending and provision across the country, from a maximum of £100 per head to a minimum of £30 while ratios of workers to young people varied from 1:266 to 1:4,900. These figures have improved marginally since (Merton et al., 2005) and a standard of 1:400 has been set in *Resourcing Excellent Youth Services* (DfES/Connexions, 2002). It also confirmed the shift to short term funding based on targeting groups of young people and joint working with other agencies.

There was still no sign of the promised legislation and the rapid changes in the ministers in charge did not bode well for a long term strategy. It became obvious that nothing was going to happen for the youth service outside the social exclusion agenda (see Chapter 8, Mizen, 2003; Wylie, 2004). The government wanted an increased emphasis on work with 'disaffected or 'excluded' young people and more partnership working with other agencies.

The government's Social Exclusion Unit (SEU) was set up in December 1997, the idea being that it could deal with concerns that spanned government departments and develop new policies for them (Wylie, 2004).

Connexions

In 1999 the SEU studied the position of those young people aged 16–18 who were not in education, training or employment, and produced *Bridging the Gap* (SEU, 1999). The report led to *Connexions: The Best Start in Life for Every Young Person* (DfES, 2002) which proposed a solution to the problems of poor achievement, disaffection and unemployment in the setting up of a new 'Youth Support Service' with Connexions partnerships in every area. Since April 2003 these have been operating nationally, having incorporated the careers service and parts of the youth service.

Personal advisors were created, employed by partnerships to work with young people individually, every young person between the ages of 13 and 18 is supposed to have a personal advisor but priority is given to those most in need of help (particularly those over 16 and not in education, employment or training). The role of the personal advisor is not only to ensure that young people take up education, training or employment opportunities, but also to help them to address factors such as drug abuse or problems at home.

Wylie (2004) describes how the arrival of Connexions presented the youth service with some difficult choices, particularly 'how to deliver locally accessible youth provision, of the kind young people say they want, and their own space to meet friends'. I assume he means youth clubs but he doesn't use the term, describing the requirement as, 'informal leisure and recreation shaped by an explicit concern for the personal and social development of those participating' (Wylie, 2004: 25).

The Policy Action Team Report (PAT, 12: 2000) highlighted the need for improved community facilities and a focus on prevention with a budget to promote cross-cutting interventions for young people at risk. But by then the government was initiating Connexions. The report did lead to the creation of a Minister for Children and Young People and a Children and Young People's Unit.

Transforming Youth Work

Transforming Youth Work was published in 2001 by the DfEE and Connexions Unit under the purple Connexions banner. While welcomed in the field as a sign that the government was at least interested at last, its vision of the service was greeted with dismay by some; 'It's narrowing and mediocre vision is the triumph of a self-serving and bureaucratic imagination' (Smith, 2002). Smith also felt it re-oriented the youth service towards an emphasis on surveillance and control and the Joseph Rowntree Foundation commented:

> *There is also a danger that quality becomes synonymous with formal outputs and accreditation. The provision of social opportunities, meeting space and constructive time for young people to share thoughts, ideas and set their own agenda must not be lost in the drive to improve standards.*
>
> (Joseph Rowntree Foundation response to *Transforming Youth Work*)

In launching *Transforming Youth Work* the Minister said the new Connexions service could not be delivered without 'vibrant and high quality youth work'. The paper proposed a new common planning framework for local authorities, a self-assessment process to inform an annual report on youth services, and a follow up programme for OFSTED inspections. It welcomed the NYA's Youth Service Pledge but didn't give any spending guidance. The document talked about keeping young people in 'good shape', a very narrow definition of well-being, and it built on the shift to targeted issue-based work that was evident through the 1990s.

Resourcing Excellent Youth Services

In the final strand of the *Transforming Youth Work* initiative, the government produced a report, *Resourcing Excellent Youth Services* (2002) which laid out for the first time what government thinks local authorities, in partnership with young people and the voluntary sector, should provide by way of youth services. The government now has the power to intervene to improve poorly performing services and qualitative and quantitative standards have now been defined to ensure that they provide 'an adequate and sufficient service'. The Government Minister, Ivan Lewis, says it 'effectively puts youth work on a statutory footing'. More money has been given (5.9 per cent) but, more importantly, the local authorities can now be made to spend it on the youth service. This should lead to a more even service level across the country: staggering differences in funding still exist throughout the country, from £228 a head to £28 (National Youth Agency audit data, YPN: 26.3.03).

There are 22 standards which must be met by 2005 which do include 'a wide diversity of youth clubs, projects and youth activities' and an aim to contact 25 per cent of those aged 13–19. However, the drive to measurable outcomes (*Transforming Youth Work*, DfEE, 2001) may change the whole face of the work. This has inspired some services, like Gloucestershire, to set up their own 'in house' system (YPN, 3.9.03) of accreditation while others continue to use the Duke of Edinburgh's Award or the Asdan Youth Award schemes (NYA, 2003).

A speech by the Minister for Young People and Learning (Lewis, 2001) described a project in his constituency which provides a safe and secure drop-in environment with various organised activities and an advice and information point. However, he went on to describe the service as focusing on 'hard to reach' young people and being concerned with 'keeping young people in good shape'. He highlighted examples of young people acquiring measurable skills. He wanted to see youth workers undertaking the 'personal advisor' role across all their activities. Although Lewis was clear that he did not want to see the youth service integrated into Connexions, the policy does require that all work with 13–19-year-olds is integral to the Connexions service and its objectives and that the youth service is a key partner in its delivery. If the youth service is to be judged on the Connexions criteria of numbers of young people in education, training or employment and a reduction in teenage pregnancy, drug use and juvenile crime then it is being judged on something it was not set up to do. The Connexions strategy does not address the need for young people to become part of groups and networks and join clubs.

As Smith states:

> *. . . the specification substantially increases the pressure to formalise the activities of workers within youth services and to take them away from the sorts of open-ended conversations, activities and relationships that defined the work in the twentieth century.*
>
> (www.infoed.co.uk)

While more funding has been coming into the service, some services are now so bound up with Connexions it is difficult to differentiate these funds and they do not seem to be going to the voluntary sector which had experienced declining support from local authorities in the previous decade (Shaw, 2003).

Youth management

Another government policy involving youth workers was outlined in the *Respect and Responsibility* White Paper and implemented in the legislation setting up Anti-Social Behaviour Orders. While acknowledging the importance of youth work in getting young people to engage with their communities, it also draws youth workers into the enforcement end and a 'youth management' role. The service is involved in dealing with anti-social behaviour by being part of 'crime and disorder reduction partnerships'.

Youth development

Much youth work is now described as youth development. In recent issues of *Young People Now*, posts for youth development workers predominate over those for youth workers. This term seems to have crept in with *Transforming Youth Work* and Connexions. Smith (2003) thinks it is really more akin to social work than to youth work in that the voluntary participation of the young people is not necessarily a core principle.

Children's Trusts

Following on from the *Every Child Matters* White Paper (2003) the government has announced the formation of Children's Trusts in every local authority by 2008. These will encompass all local authority services for children and young people, and there has been much criticism of their name, while the Minister has now suggested trusts will be able to add 'and young people' to their name. This is thought by some to herald the end of distinct youth services as we know them (YPN, 11–16 June 2004).

Funding was also announced for Children's Centres (*Children Now*, 5–11 May 2004) which will bring together childcare and early education, health and family support, employment and other services, but no mention of funding for youth centres.

The 'Youth Offer' Green Paper

This was announced in the document *Five Year Strategy for Children and Learners* published by the Department for Education and Skills in July 2004 (www.dfes.gov.uk). The Department for Education and Skills acknowledges there is a lack of interesting, accessible and affordable things to do for young people. It says it will create more opportunities that enable young people to get involved in their communities but also provide more places where they can simply go and enjoy themselves, so maybe we will see a resurgence of youth clubs! However, writing in the TES (30.7.04) Shaw felt the paper was about shifting the burden of supporting 'challenging teenagers' from schools to other agencies. The idea of 'extended schools' open early and late is suggested. Young people should get support to help them address risks, take part in 'exciting and enjoyable' personal and social development activities in and out of school, get high quality careers advice and a chance to influence the services they receive. The paper will build on the Children Bill creating Children's Trusts. Smith (2004) feels that, while the strategy is 'riddled with a concern for skilling and accreditation' there are some countervailing pressures arising out of evidence surrounding the membership of clubs and the cultivation of social capital (see Chapter 8). However, he also suggests there may be pressure to convert the focus of youth centres to younger children, especially with the government's aim of establishing a Children's Centre in every community.

The future

In my concluding Chapter 8 I will attempt to examine whether youth clubs can still have a future in the light of these seismic changes.

Chapter 3

The Role of Adults

This chapter looks at who is involved in providing and supporting youth clubs and the roles played by full and part-time youth workers, cleaners and caretakers, volunteers, parents and senior members, and elected members of the local authority. The role of members of management committees and workers from other agencies are discussed in the chapter on management, Chapter 6. The second half of the chapter looks at making relationships, being a role model and the different styles that workers adopt.

Youth club workers

The most important thing is that workers enjoy being with young people and want to be there:

> *The best youth workers were seen as those who were friendly, approachable, had a sense of humour, and were tolerant of the members. The worst were strict or bossy and tried to impose their own standards on the young people.*
>
> (Furlong et al., 1998)

Most youth club workers enjoy it, and if they don't they should find another job. Young people soon know who wants to be there and who is clock watching, although sometimes all youth workers want to be somewhere else!

Although the idea of a youth leader has been superseded by that of a youth worker it must be true that in an institution like a youth club 'The person or character of the worker is of fundamental importance' as Brew (1947) affirms. Youth workers also need to be able to show empathy skills, listening skills and skills in building trust (Wheal, 1998). Many adults have these qualities, and can develop the skills. Traditionally part-time workers have been recruited from the local area; the majority of them being women who often undertook training. Some part-time workers then took up full-time training, but for most it remained an absorbing and important part-time interest. The hourly rate often compared well with other part-time work but most put in over and above their paid hours, often working at weekends etc. Only recently have they been paid for time spent in training or supervision.

The NYB estimated in 1983 that the number of part-time workers in the statutory service (including grant aided voluntary organisations) was 28,300. By 1998 the NYA Audit recorded the figure to be down to about 24,000 (in addition to the 3,200 full-time workers). At present there is a problem with recruiting both full and part-time workers (Ghose, 2002) and many posts have to be re-advertised. In a 2001 survey done by Bracknell Forest Council (YPN 12.02.03) 94 per cent of youth services had trouble filling part-time vacancies. There may be many reasons (see Chapter 8) why this involvement in the local community has declined in the UK much as it has in America (Putnam, 2000). For instance, more women are working full-time, it is not worth it for people on benefits, there is less unemployment but people are working longer hours (people in England work the longest hours in Europe). However, part of the problem may be the high expectations placed on part-time workers not only to *do* the work but also to *monitor* and *record* it. Clubs in the voluntary sector also struggle to recruit and there is a reluctance from adults to take on roles in village or one night a week clubs. Issues of responsibility, a culture inclined to litigation and enhanced criminal record checks may be issues here.

Following the Cullen Report, suspicions about the suitability of people wanting to work with young people have led to the implementation of much more stringent background checks, with the criminal records bureau (CRB) being set up. Indeed everyone involved with young people, even school governors for example, have to do this. The disclosure of potential abusers is of course vital but there must be a way of doing this without putting people off from volunteering, maybe because they may have committed a minor offence in their youth, and don't wish it generally known.

Cleaners and caretakers

A good relationship with the cleaner or caretaker is very important. The youth worker should make every effort to encourage the young people to put away equipment and clean up after themselves. In an age when many children don't wash up or do any tidying or cleaning at home this can be extremely difficult! In my first full-time club I used to drive round the block if I arrived at the club and saw the cleaners were still there – especially if we had been doing pottery or cooking the night before!

The person responsible for cleaning the building may well have a remit that goes beyond simple tidying and cleaning and include responsibility for opening up and locking up. However, the youth worker may well need to open up and lock up themselves as, although there may be a responsible caretaker, it is rare to find one employed to work evenings or weekends even in large centres nowadays.

Clerical staff

In full-time youth centres there should be clerical help to free youth workers from financial and administrative tasks, which are not usually their forte. The budget for this is often separate from part-time youth work and often not seen as so important but it is a crucial support to youth club workers and the clerical workers may become very involved in the life of the centre, encouraging young people to pop in for a chat and ending up doing youth work themselves. In small part-time clubs there may be someone who would do clerical work for the club, and this type of help is invaluable. Sometimes senior members may be keen to get involved in keeping the books, typing letters etc.

Volunteers

The Thompson Report (1982) estimated that there were over 500,000 volunteers in the youth service. Eighty per cent were in voluntary organisations but that still left a large number in the statutory sector. In line with many full-timers, much of the voluntary work done in youth clubs is by paid part-timers giving their time free outside their normal working hours. But other volunteers are always needed and, despite it being a vital part of any youth workers job the recruitment and support of volunteers has often been neglected. It is increasingly difficult to find volunteers for all youth work – there is a waiting list for the Girl Guides for example because of a lack of leaders.

Parents

Parents are another important source of volunteer help, especially in small one night a week clubs. However, older young people may resent or be embarrassed by their parents involvement, seeing the club as a 'parent free' space.

Parents may sometimes be reluctant to be involved in the activities of the club but in small voluntary clubs, parents will often have initiated and be running the club. Rotas for parental involvement can be helpful, as they may not want to come along every week – but one night in six doesn't seem so bad. For small rural clubs, the transport provided by the parents, not only to bring young people to the club, but to go ten pin bowling etc, is the only thing that makes these activities possible.

Parents will often be keen to support their children at competitions, but it is usually easier to recruit volunteers from parents of seven-year-olds than fourteen-year-olds. Someone once described this as the Kevin Kegan phenomenon, probably now the David Beckham phenomenon. Dads think their seven-year-old could become a top footballer, by the time they are fourteen they know they won't! It is important to try and maintain good relationships with parents, involving them wherever possible, perhaps on the management committee and they will certainly usually be happy to turn up to fundraising or social events. Dramatic productions will usually bring parents in to watch their offspring perform and a video showing of the holiday scheme we undertook was a big success, if rather drawn out with everyone watching their child abseil off the quarry wall. One particular child took about twenty minutes to decide to do it!

Senior members

Some young people who have been involved in the club for a long time will often want to take a leadership role in the club. In the step model of curriculum development (Huskins, 1996: 25) young people move through stages in their involvement in the club. He describes young people moving from contact, through socialising and being involved, to leadership. Of course, not all members of a youth club will want to continue their involvement in this way but the minority who do will respond to the idea of taking more responsibility as senior members, helping to run the junior club, organising activities. Many clubs are very good at retaining young people and encourage them to undertake training. Senior member training initiatives are run by many local authorities and by national associations, for example, the National Association of Clubs for Young People runs an Effective Leadership course, bringing together young people from affiliated clubs all over the country and using outdoor activities to engender team building and encourage leadership skills. There can surely be no better advertisement for youth club work than for young people who have developed personally through the club to want to help other young people to do so and many go on to become part-time, and indeed full-time youth club workers themselves. Young people often see this as a way to give something back (Bradford, 2004).

Ex-members

Ex-members of the club are a potential source of management committee members and volunteers and many will be keen to support their club. Many of the large voluntary clubs (Rose, 1998) rely heavily on this source for staffing and general help with repairs etc. However, they may need to realise that times have changed. Maybe they did go on the annual club outing to Blackpool every year, and were grateful, but it may not fulfil the needs of young people in the club now.

Elected council members

I was amazed when I worked in County Council offices, at the priority that was given to the questions and requests of local authority councillors. Officers can be asked to drop everything else to respond to a request for information or a complaint from an elected member – these are potentially powerful people! There is no doubt that having elected members on your side can be of enormous benefit. It is a good idea to involve council members in the management committee, invite them to club events and keep them regularly updated. For one thing if local residents want to complain about the club, young people's behaviour etc., it's often the local councillor who will hear it first. The youth service is one of the areas over which councillors still exercise strategic direction – as schools are so autonomous, and youth services often enjoy good relationships with members visiting projects regularly (Merton et al., 2005).

How to influence young people

As Button (1974) suggests, if youth workers are not there to influence young people what are they there for? There are many different ways of having this influence and there is no one type of youth worker. All workers however act as role models to a certain extent, even if young people turn against the model rather than copy it.

Role models

In 1890 Maud Stanley advised that 'workers must have a dignity in themselves; to command respect, even tempered, show no favouritism, and be friendly and lively and tactful'.

Being a role model can be regarded as an educational method (Rosseter, 1987) in that young people change by modelling their characteristics on those of the worker. Certainly it is good for young people to be exposed to different ways of life and of being than usually surround them; women workers have always been keen to break down sex role stereotypes. This was one of the reasons I learnt to instruct in rock climbing. It is important that the club shows men and women out of their traditional roles, male staff helping with cookery for example, and having disabled and black staff in the club offers young people positive role models to identify with. In *The Art of Youth Work* (1999) Kerry Young gives examples of the influence workers can have:

> *. . . she was the only Asian Youth worker I knew and I thought that was wonderful because she was like a role model, so I sort of do similar things like not judging people and giving them a chance.*
>
> (p89)

Truman and Brent (1995) quote a young person:

> *I modelled myself on X, I always asked myself what he would have done in a given situation.*

It is important that young people have different models to choose from in their lives. Young people often have very fixed views about how adults should behave and will not hesitate to be critical of workers life style or appearance. I once reduced a group of girls to hysterics by appearing in a floral skirt and, on a more serious note, inspired some real animosity by leaving my small baby to work in a girls' residential home, where many of the residents felt they had been abandoned by *their* mothers. These personal interactions can be very challenging and how much each youth worker wants to expose of themselves will vary considerably.

Youth workers can supply a model of future relationships with adults, as an adult who relates to them in a different way, and has no fixed agenda in their lives. However, youth workers must be careful about assuming too much influence; young people meet many other people in the course of a day. The way staff behave to each other and to the young people is extremely important and while it is easy to 'lose it' when tired or provoked, it is important to acknowledge that your behaviour was unacceptable in the same way as we would expect young people to apologise. Treating young people in an adult fashion will encourage them to behave as adults and not to react as children. Transactional analysis (Berne, 1972) is a useful concept which makes us think about the way we relate to each other.

Making relationships

> *From every person one meets in a lifetime a little is gained and retained for one's own personal use.*
>
> (Maugham, quoted in Rose, 1998: 129)

One of the most important things that young people get from youth clubs is the relationships they make with adults. For some the relationship with a youth worker may be the closest adult relationship they have. They appreciate youth workers for someone to talk to, not necessarily to give advice but often just to listen. It could be described as 'coffee bar counselling'. Youth clubs can be an important source of information and advice for many young people who may not have other avenues to obtain it. Williamson (1997) found that young people felt that youth workers did not preach at them but understood and empathised and above all were trustworthy. They were there for them no matter what, and did not need to know all the answers. Certainly the informal nature of the youth work relationship means that workers have to gain trust by demonstrating their trustworthiness; young people quickly find out who they can confide in. Young people talk about being given respect, listened to and treated as adults as an important aspect of the relationship. Relationships with youth workers were rated highly compared to those with teachers in research done with young people in youth clubs in Nottingham for the National Association of Clubs for Young People 'she is like a second mum' (Bradford, 2004) and the Impact of Youth Work research (Merton et al., 2005).

Making relationships is one of the fundamental tasks of any youth worker. The wonderful thing about relationships made with young people in a youth club setting is that they are voluntary, at least in the sense that the young people have chosen to be there, and have the potential to be deep and lasting. This quality of relationship alone can justify this type of work. In *Kids at the Door Revisited* (Holman, 2000), Bob Holman went back to talk to young people that he had worked with several years previously. He wanted to find out what effect the experience had had on them. Above all what came over was the importance of the club for young people, both as a place of refuge and safety, but also as the place where they made relationships with adults on an equal footing. Long-term bases also enable short-term projects to work. The Southmead youth worker, Jeremy Brent cites an example of a 'terrific short term arts project' in Southmead in 1996, with an exhibition of energetic and colourful paintings called 'Fresh Evidence' at the city arts gallery. This was very popular (visited by thousands), and critically acclaimed, but could not have happened without the long-term existence of the youth centre. Many workers, including Brent, have worked in a youth club for many years and provide a fixed point in young people's lives.

Young (1999) likens the relationship between the worker and the young person to the foundation of a house; if it is not firmly established then the walls and ceiling will collapse. Relationships form the basis for young people's development and empowerment. Smith (2002) illustrates the need for these relationships to be 'authentic' i.e. the relationship must be real and genuine for both young person and adult worker. She argues that working with people is all about working in the grey areas, with no clear blueprints, and feels that an emphasis on targets, boundaries and set ways of working should be questioned as it puts obstacles in the way of workers connecting genuinely with young people. Jeffs (1997) argues that recent concentration on short-term funding has meant that workers have been unable to create long-term relationships; they have to target specific groups and impose themselves on them to get outcomes. This was the problem I was confronted with while managing a Youth Action Scheme project in Gloucestershire, we were under pressure to show that our interventions kept young people out of trouble when we had often only spent a week on a residential with them.

However sure we are that relationships are central to youth work, it is also the aspect most difficult to quantify. Writing from his experience as a centre based worker, Richardson (1997) feels that young people need stability in relationships. He sees the youth centre as a place to meet, to work together and develop a sense of community. In a helping relationship, both parties – youth worker and young person – are helped, changed and encouraged. The relationship starts by an attempt to understand the lives of young people in the community and with a positive attitude towards them. This is shown by a young person's verdict on 'Kids Company' a drop in centre in London (*The Guardian*, 29.01.03). 'Here, you receive love. It is the first time in my life I got support.' Research by Hendry et al. (1993) showed that the most valued quality in adults, according to young people, was a belief in the young person.

Making relationships with young people comes more easily to some adults than others, but if you are really interested in the young people and want to get to know them, you are half-way there. It's always possible to find common points of reference, even if you don't like the music and hate football. It's very important to remember names, so workers need to develop a skill in this; using their name every time you see a young person during the evening helps, along with finding something out about them that you can refer to, a hobby, pet, their family, school etc.

Relationships need to be nurtured and can take a long time to develop although, as Button suggests (1971) young people are often willing to have deep conversations even if they have only just met the worker if treated with respect. In a youth club an adult is in young people's space and if they are having a conversation you can't assume you have a right to join in. Youth clubs allow young people a 'foot in both camps' (Hendry et al., 1993). They can associate with adults on a regular basis but also continue to align themselves with their peers and therefore develop a variety of social roles.

Style

The youth worker in charge of a club, whether on a full, part-time or voluntary basis has a very important role to play. The following section explores different styles of leadership. However, very few workers will conform to one type all the time. Lippett and White's (1960) classic work on leadership styles (often used in management studies) examines the role of a leader with a group of boys undertaking an activity. The types of role which the worker took 'democratic', 'laissez faire' and 'authoritarian' were examined to see how useful they were to the completion of a task. The democratic style was ultimately most effective in achieving a task, as the boys worked together even when the worker was not there. There was more originality, group-mindedness and friendliness in democratic groups. In contrast, there was more aggression, hostility, scapegoating and discontent in laissez-faire and autocratic groups (Lewin, 1948; Lippett and White, 1960). Nearly everyone will become authoritarian faced with certain situations, but it is not a helpful approach in the long run if you are aiming for participation and empowerment.

Laissez-faire basically means 'do what you like'. It may sometimes look as though some youth clubs are run like this, but it is usually used as an insult! Youth workers who want young people to become involved may try to step back and do nothing, but it is usually a recipe for disaster as young people need boundaries and are not experienced in how to behave without them. The aim of most youth workers is to get from an authoritarian state, where they hold the keys and make the rules, to a democratic situation where decisions are taken by the group as a whole. As educators, youth workers aim to manage and control the learning of young people (Jeffs and Smith, 1999) and this means workers have to intervene and use discipline in certain situations (see Chapter 4).

Social architect

Button's (1974) description of youth workers in centres acting as social architects is extremely useful. Young people gather together in youth clubs groups of their own choosing and it is through these groups that the youth worker seeks to have an influence. Button felt that:

> *. . . the youth worker responsible for a large organisation is inevitably a group worker, as his main instrument of influence is through groups of various kinds and what these groups do together.*
>
> (1974: 130)

The structure of these groups and their relationship to the whole can be very complex. The groups can be friendship groups, task groups, or associate groups and individuals will probably move between several groups during the course of an evening session. Button suggests that, within this setting, the youth worker serves as a social architect – the worker will influence the situation whatever they do. The choice of the youth worker is whether to be a skilled architect and work knowingly. Button looks at how the youth worker can reach individual young people in the youth club, and affect their development through work done with them in small groups. Much of this work would be done by part-time or volunteer staff, so that the training and commitment of these staff becomes paramount. They also need good supervision. Button criticises workers who fail to challenge and try to change unhelpful group norms operating in their clubs. For him, a youth worker is clearly an educator and must help groups to break free from unhelpful controls. It may be difficult to change young people's attitudes, because they are mixed up with their personality or they are reinforced by the climate around them. Encouraging responsible behaviour can often be best done at a tangent by not looking at the actual behaviour but engaging young people in consultation, a method that would often be described as action research today. Button (1974) gives examples of the sort of enquiries that could be undertaken, into their own communities or into other people's problems.

Leader

To be ruler of a small kingdom can make youth work attractive to some. Signs saying 'Leader, Keep Out' on office doors betray this type. It's important not to use the youth club as an arena for autocratic power over staff and young people, or as a place to show off your superior pool or table tennis skills. Showing the young people how to get involved is a good use of leadership skills; when workshops are put on in centres the enthusiasm of the worker to get involved can encourage young people to try something they would not have done otherwise, such as dance or drama.

There is also a need for a full-time youth worker to be a team leader, as Henriques wrote in 1933:

> *To direct the activities, organise the whole work, and satisfy himself that it is being carried out efficiently and satisfactorily he must coordinate all efforts made by his helpers, the officers and the boys, and see that all are working harmoniously and happily together.*
>
> (p.61)

Friend

Some youth workers just never grew up and while joining in youth club activities or indulging your 'free child', as Berne (1972) calls it is, undoubtedly, a good thing in its place, it is important that relationships with young people do not become inappropriate. For example, some young people will always want to hang around the worker, lacking the confidence to join a group, but it is the job of a youth worker to help young people to make friends with each other, not to become a substitute friend. Maud Stanley recognised this in 1890 (Booton, 1985) when she advised that 'ill bred familiarity' be discouraged!

Manager

The worker in charge has a pivotal role as they will be managing the other staff besides working face to face with young people. It is hard to overestimate the difficulty of this role: the worker must never lose sight of the fact that their primary purpose is to support young people in the use of the centre. Unfortunately, due to financial pressures, some workers have been persuaded that a badminton class will not only bring in hard needed cash, but also give them a much needed night off. Many full-time workers have now been so over-burdened with daytime responsibilities, interagency meetings, school work etc. that many so called full-time centres are now only open for youth work on two or three nights a week (Bamber, 2000). These centres were designed to be the hub of the leisure time activities for the young people of the area, a place where they could meet regularly. In a large full-time centre there are enormous pressures, but even in a one night a week club the youth worker will need to organise a programme and involve other adults. Youth workers should not be found in the office in the evenings – one of the classic signs of the manager role taking over! Staff supervision and support is important but when the youth club is open staff need support out there, and to have a role model of how to do face to face work. The full-time worker, or part-time worker in charge, may often be the only worker who has received any training and so part of their role is to coach others and lead by example.

Redcoat

This approach was defined by Foreman (1987) likening youth workers to the organisers at Butlins holiday camps known as 'Redcoats'. She is disparaging about youth workers as redcoats. She feels there is a fundamental incompatibility between the roles of youth worker and redcoat, as redcoats only require the presence of young people in order to get them involved and entertained, while youth workers require an appreciation of the social and political influences that affect their situation. Foreman wants youth workers to be seen as educators, but being a redcoat can be educative: if one of young people's educational and developmental needs is for new experiences. One of the problems with a redcoat style is that many youth workers aren't very good at it and also feel decidedly guilty about organising activities themselves, as they have been taught that the ideas are supposed to come from the young people. These attitudes have often produced a situation where young people have nothing to do and become bored. In my view, it is far worse to have a youth club where there is nothing going on than one where there is too much organisation. Workers generally should aim for a balance with young people being involved in organising the details of activities, within an overall framework.

Counsellor

Some workers like nothing better than to work with young people on an individual basis. However, it is important that workers don't get carried away and refer to themselves as counsellors unless they are trained to do it. It is also important that young people understand that, particularly in relation to child abuse, there are issues around confidentiality (Banks, 1999). The centre based worker should refer a young person for specialist counselling if this is what is needed or to social services. However, it is undoubtedly true that the relationship many young people build up with youth workers will lead them to confide in them and ask for their advice. All youth workers should know where to access information and be able to provide a listening ear, but if workers want to spend all their time working one to one with young people, they should maybe look for a different job.

Preserver of the heritage

Youth workers who have been involved in the youth club 'man and boy' for the last 50 years often like it as it is and don't like change. While getting to know the area and establishing relationships takes time, sometimes workers miss the right time to move on and then become reluctant to. They may then want to preserve the club as it was in its heyday. Valuable community resources can become tied up in institutions which are not really catering for the needs of young people in the area. Of course it is the youth officer's role to engineer change, but many workers will be supported by their management committees in wanting to keep things as they were.

Hearty

This description comes from Mary Blandy's excellent book about a youth club in the 1960s (Blandy, 1967). The hearty was a worker who tried to enthuse young people by his own over vigorous approach. Bearded and wearing shorts, he was very much into activities, usually outdoors and uncomfortable! Undoubtedly these sorts of workers often manage to engage young people in activities they would never have dreamt of doing otherwise. However, it is important that workers think about whose needs they are meeting – hopefully both their own and the young peoples. Nevertheless, it is valid that youth workers get something personal from the job.

What workers get out of it

To be able to get out of the house and away from your own kids and the TV, spend your evenings in a warm friendly place where you can meet new people and make new friends, learn new skills or pursue your hobby – and get paid! What job could be better! It is still true that, for many, youth work is a vocation – this does not provide a good excuse for it not being paid properly, but many people go into the work from a sense of vocation. There are many Christian youth workers in both the church and state sectors of youth work and many from other faiths. Socialism and feminism propelled some workers into youth work (Taylor, 1989). I went into it partly from a desire to change the world, or at least a small bit of it. Being able to work in the evening when my small child had gone to bed was another attraction for me and it was always great not to have to be in work early in the morning. It's a job for owls not larks! The autonomy of youth work was another attraction. Unfortunately, the current pressures on full-time workers leave them little autonomy and many work longer hours in the daytime, and often fewer face-to-face hours, or work too many hours altogether! It seems that recently, many qualified full-time workers are not seeking to work in clubs. However, there are still workers out there who have been in the job for many years and remain enthusiastic (*Young People Now*, 6.8.03). The role of full-time youth club worker is not valued sufficiently within or outside the service, and there are increasing opportunities available in other professions such as learning mentors, youth justice workers, personal advisors. However, I personally had the opportunity to try many new activities through youth work, had some great times with young people, and can still play an OK game of pool and table tennis! What is also rewarding is that youth club life is unpredictable. Even on a wet Wednesday night, someone can decide to tell you a secret or someone can be hit by a pool cue and you'll be in hospital with them for the next few hours!

Chapter 4

Good Practice in Youth Club Work

Having fun

One of the main aims of a youth club must be to have fun. A club after all is a voluntary commitment for young people, who have many other choices in their lives. If we want them to choose us, not just because there is nowhere else to go, but because they relax after school, meet their friends, have new experiences, make useful relationships with adults and experience informal education, then we must aim to make the whole experience a positive one from coming through the door to leaving at the end of the evening. This chapter looks at how this can be done, starting with the importance of informal education and examining atmosphere and access, curriculum, activities, issues, discipline and participation. The chapter ends with some inspiring stories about clubs.

The building – atmosphere and access

> *On entering the club, members should get a feeling of warm hospitality, whilst the environment should be friendly and relaxed it must also be gay and stimulate the curiosity.*
>
> (Ministry of Education Building Bulletin No. 20, 1963: 13)

The language may be archaic but the premise is correct – youth clubs should be attractive to young people. It is a good idea for workers to stand back occasionally and look at the club as though they had never seen it before, or ask a new arrival to comment. Are the posters up to date or has that event already happened? Are there events planned and advertised? Photos of members and staff on club activities help to give a sense of ownership: the choice of décor, production of murals and so on all help. There should be music of course, but not to drown out any attempts at conversation. After all it's important that young people realise that conversation is one of the reasons they are there. The place should be warm (I once pulled out of an interview at a club as it was so cold!) – staff need to be comfortable or they won't want to come to work. Young people can warm up rushing around, but warmth is another factor in inviting young people in and encouraging conversation. Any building must be warm, dry, clean and accessible (Myhill, 1985). One of the main problems with youth club work today is the quality of premises that workers have to operate within. While there are notable exceptions such as the new Emmanuel project in Forest Gate, east London which opened in May 2003 (White, 2003), and is described as 'cool' by its members, most purpose built centres were built for the purposes of the 1960s, not today. For example the Ofsted report on Bristol Youth Service (2000) found that:

> *Buildings are generally in poor condition and require major investment over a period of time to bring them up to a standard that reflects the value the service places on young people. Too many buildings hinder work because of inadequate heating. Furnishings and fittings are in a very poor condition and provide a very poor environment for youth work.*

Young people are generally dissatisfied with the buildings they have to meet in (Merton et al., 2005). However, it is possible to improve the environment quite cheaply by the young people doing it themselves and the Bristol Ofsted report also found that 'where young people have been involved in the decoration of the premises, particularly the painting of murals, there is a greater feeling of belonging and of responsibility'.

Whilst this is true, young people could still get this by planning the work for other people to do and much of the work needed in our older centres needs experts. For too long we have encouraged young people to paper over the cracks rather than campaigning, with them, for up to date facilities.

One of the reasons there are so many old buildings run by the youth service is that the many adult groups who use them often lobby hard for their retention. While I am in favour of buildings for young people it would probably often be a better use of resources to have a smaller building which did not need so much maintenance, and could be made more user friendly, than some of these great barns of places which the adult community value to play badminton in or have tea dances. However, disposing of buildings is no easy matter when there may be many parties involved, for example in Portishead (YPN, 27.08.03) the building is owned by one council, but the land is owned by another and the building is actually leased to the voluntary management committee! Also council members tend often to be very parochial and will support having an old building retained on their patch rather than a new one on someone else's only a mile away, this makes the role of the youth officer in strategic planning very difficult.

Voluntary attendance

One of the major points of discussion in youth work is the notion of voluntary attendance, and whether it is fundamental to youth work. It is certainly the basis of club work. Young people come to youth clubs because they want to come. However, what makes a club attractive is debatable. Young people won't necessarily flood in because there is new furniture. As Mary Blandy (1967) describes, a good club atmosphere could still function in spartan premises. One of the best clubs I worked in for atmosphere was a prefab originally put up as a temporary school classroom. The gas heaters had metal guards with huge dents in the middle where everyone sat and the donated old sofas and sagging armchairs made the atmosphere cosy. The main thing is that young people are made to feel welcome and that it is their space. It is important that when someone comes in they are spoken to, and made to feel welcome by a member of staff, or young person.

Reception

The reception area in a club is very important, as it is the first place young people come to, and must be welcoming. The reception area and the coffee bar are also areas where anyone feeling a bit lost will hang around, so it's a good place to have conversations and always has been.

On the first night I worked in a full-time club, I was waiting on reception in some trepidation for the members to arrive. As the door was opened they rushed in shouting numbers at me, 25, 14, 46! The membership system there had run on a number basis and it took me a while to persuade people to give me their names. I've also experienced clubs where the door has to be unlocked to let individuals in, and where no-one seems interested whether they have come in or not. One wonders why they bother. For many it's because there is nowhere else to go in the area – not really voluntary attendance.

Access can be seen as actual physical access to the building as well as more subtle questions about opening times, entrance fees, lighting, location etc. Physical accessibility is important, too many clubs today are still not wheelchair accessible, or access is round the back or there is a whole upstairs section that is inaccessible. Equal opportunities issues are dealt with in more detail in Chapter 5.

Health and safety

Health and safety is an important consideration in building based work. Each trade union branch will have a health and safety officer who should check each building (Nicholls, 2002). At the end of the day, it is the club leader's responsibility to make sure the premises and the activities undertaken are safe and if they are not, or there are not enough staff to ensure this, the building should not be opened. However, life with young people can never be risk free. Management supervision and support for workers is vital, workers who try new things with young people may well have difficulties, but young people need an element of adventure and risk in their lives.

Opening times

Opening times can also be discriminatory, for example as some young people may not be allowed out in the evening and girls clubs often work well as an after school provision. Many clubs are away from main streets and young people may be understandably anxious about approaching them in the dark. It is important that lighting lights not only the entrance but the path and area around: it may well be a risky situation for a youth worker locking up a building on their own late at night in the dark. Many young people would like youth clubs to be open later at night than the usual 9.30 or 10 p.m., but staff are not usually keen to work much later, at least not on a regular basis.

It's worth thinking about meeting earlier in the winter months, like after school or offering somewhere to do homework. Being open at times that young people want to come implies evenings, but it may mean day times or weekends or holidays. The trend over recent years, to curtail the number of hours of opening and the number of nights, is saddening.

Transport

Although The NYA Youth Work Pledge states that all young people should have a warm place to meet a bus ride away this is still not the case for many young people, particularly in rural areas and city bus services are not always reliable in the evenings. Young people may often be dependent on parents for transport as parents may have worries about them being out at night and coming home by themselves, even where there is a bus, or its not far to walk.

Numbers

It should really be possible, and sensible in view of the cost of buildings, to have a building open all year. Perhaps in the holidays, daytime provision will work best, but it is important that workers and managers look at their attendance and change the programme when necessary. If the club is suddenly quiet on a Thursday because a local disco has started an under 16s night it might be better to shut up and go over there and open on a different night, or at least change the staffing. For these reasons it is important to monitor attendance. Youth workers will often argue that the best youth work is done in small groups, but in terms of atmosphere in a club that encourages interaction and enables several activities and groups to take place at the same time, you need numbers. Young people need to be offered a choice of activity in a club, ranging from physical games or activities such as dance, art and craft and board games, to conversation and discussion groups. One of the reasons for a club after all is to encourage a range of young people to come and interact with each other. For association you need a reasonably large number of people to associate with, and workers must not be complacent about low attendance – it needs investigating.

Charging

Whether or not to charge for admittance, and how much, is a difficult decision. The fee often puts young people off and leads to all those 'I was only popping in to see if Fred's here' situations, besides it often ties up a member of staff on cash extrication duty all night. Young people often seem less willing to pay in large local authority clubs; they feel that the council provides this anyway. Entrance fees provide a useful source of club revenue, and may be the main source in voluntary clubs. Young people should be involved in the decision about charging and, if they decide to operate a membership or charging system then they should operate it themselves and decide how to spend the money. A long time ago in Withywood youth club it was the members committees job to collect subs and wellcome new members (Sharpe, 2004).

Curriculum

The notion of a youth work curriculum has been debated long and hard since it was first suggested by government in the early 1990s following the introduction of the National Curriculum for schools. By the time the third and last ministerial conference had met and agreed that the curriculum was about ending inequality as we know it, most local authorities had had a stab at producing a document which incorporated the central ideas of the debate: education, equality, participation and empowerment – and demonstrated how their work encompassed them. Indeed most curriculum documents, such as that produced by West Sussex, cover the whole range of youth work they undertake. In 1995 the NYA produced guidelines for developing the curriculum, *Planning the Way*. It was based around work on topics such as bullying and assertiveness. More recently, Wylie and Merton (2002) have come out with *Towards a Contemporary Curriculum.* They define curriculum as 'a selection of elements from the culture which will give people the knowledge, skills, and understanding thought necessary for work, family life, and citizenship' and go on to suggest that the youth work curriculum includes all the experiences that young people have in an organisation and allows progression to be measured. It does not however preclude spontaneity, and it seems unnecessary to keep revisiting this word when it arouses so much resistance. As a colleague of mine used to say 'If I wanted to start work at 9 a.m. I'd have been a teacher!' And if I wanted to work within something called a curriculum I would have been one too. Words are powerful symbols, and I prefer 'programmed', or 'what goes on here' or 'atmosphere' (Robertson, 2005).

'Learning outcomes' is another problematic term, as it implies we know what these will be, and young people may learn many different, and not always expected things, from participating in a youth club. Many of the important things we learn in life we learn through experience, which is why opportunities for experiential learning is also important. With experiences, we can reflect on how we felt, and learning cycles help us to benefit from experiential learning. Jeffs and Smith (1999) have produced a cycle based on the work of Lewin and Kolb. It goes from concrete experience through observation and reflection. This leads to forming abstract concepts and then testing them in new situations.

Group work is a cornerstone of youth work practice but recent research (Merton at al., 2005) found few examples of the group being used for social learning.

Group work at its best encourages reflection and allows young people to identify transferable and sustainable skills that they can use in other situations. Rock climbing is a good example of this where young people can learn to trust other people, in fact to put their lives in their friends' hands. Properly reflected on in the group, these experiences can be used to help young people think about situations where they trust other people, and where other people have to trust them. Trust exercises can also be done without rock faces of course!

Activities

Jeffs and Smith (1999) pose their question, 'what is it to be an informal educator' (p.19) and answer that 'it is about seeking to foster learning in the situations where you work, cultivating environments in which people are able to remember significant experiences, and to work at understanding them'. Creating situations where people can experience new things will also fulfill one of the developmental needs of young people. As Josephine Brew pointed out in 1943, despite their role in the development of young people, activities can often be thought of as amusement:

> *To put it crudely, people who support youth work by their money are seldom willing to support a venture which supplies nothing but what they*

> *like to call 'mere amusement'. Therefore the unfortunate leader is too often in the unenviable position of being forced to embark on a programme which shall satisfy the desire for uplift demanded by the subscribers to the club, and at the same time to cater for the club member who is not ready for this uplift and resists it to the last gasp. It is this Puritanical conception, that if people are enjoying themselves they are probably not learning anything which is at the root of much of the acknowledged dishonesty behind many annual reports.*
>
> (Brew, 1943: 49)

Young people can often be described as 'being without interests', but as Jeffs and Smith (1990) point out, this is really 'not appreciating what we like'. It is important that youth workers and young people find a common point of interest in activities.

Spence (2001) provides a useful discussion on the use of activities in youth work. She encourages us to look beyond the recreational aspects of activities to social education and the importance of the choice of activities. In 1974 Button wrote that he felt that the tradition in British youth work of offering activities to enable young people to gain 'skills, versatility, a sense of achievement, and incidentally companionship' had become less fashionable, and there was more emphasis on opportunities for young people to come together in associate groups of their own choosing. He felt that it was not obvious that young people had gained from this shift in emphasis, as the foci for interaction had become fewer and more limited. He felt that addressing the personal needs of young people needed a much more deliberate and intensive approach than many workers adopted. The job of the youth worker was not only to serve young people who needed 'remedial treatment'; it needed to offer opportunities to a range of young people to develop their own potentials. Containment rather than education was often the case in clubs. How much have things changed today?

Programming

Youth workers are educators rather than 'redcoats' as described by Forman in 1987, but this does not mean that they should not get involved in planning a programme. Youth clubs must be a place where things happen and it is the responsibility of staff to ensure that they do. If staff do not organise activities, at least initially, young people will often organise their own, which may well involve destructive behaviour. Of course it is the aim of every worker to get young people involved in organising the programme, but they need ideas and help and a role model. Youth work in the 1980s seemed to go through a phase of non-direction, which meant that youth workers had to wait for young people to come up with their own ideas. For de-motivated workers this can easily be an excuse for doing nothing. Activity breeds activity and, as Button (1975) describes 'if young people are to be given real opportunities for personal growth they need to be caught up in the kind of experience that will extend them'. He felt that the time that many young people spent in clubs was dull, repetitive and boring. Button felt that youth centres which made no demands on young people lessened their value to them, by implying that young people are not important enough to have their commitment demanded.

The activities on offer in many clubs are often the same as 30 years ago e.g. pool, table tennis, music, occasional art and craft, football and other physical activity if there is a large hall or outside area. The Space Invader machines tend to have been replaced by a computer, but many other activities can be undertaken in youth clubs such as making music, drama, creative arts and more unusual activities such as fencing, so it's important to try new, perhaps daring things. A visit to my youth club by a poet was greeted with disgust at first, followed by genuine interest and amazement that being a poet could be a job. Clubs have been able to build on young people's interest in music to develop recording studios and even radio stations.

Many ideas for club activities can be found on the internet nowadays e.g. (www.ukyouth.org.uk). In the 1980s a project called 'Youth Clubs in the 80s' set up an exchange of practice largely aimed at part-time workers. The publication that resulted, *Youth Work that Works* (NAYC, 1989) has the following themes:

- games
- going places
- communicating outside the club
- breaking down the barriers
- food
- arts and drama
- talking points
- changing the club environment

This is well worth revisiting for programme ideas. The magazine *Club Connection*, published by NACYP is full of useful ideas. Also, many of the local youth club associations, such as Young Gloucestershire and Youth Club Hampshire and Isle of Wight, employ activity leaders to bring activities to clubs, usually those difficult for clubs to organise themselves like archery or karaoke. These can be a life saver particularly for small clubs run by volunteers.

However, the programme can make itself over the course of the year, using festivals and seasonal events, such as silly games on April Fools day, pancakes and valentines in February, scary walks in the woods for Halloween, fireworks for bonfire night or Divali, pantomimes in December. Clubs with a faith background will also use religious events. Once a programme idea is successful you will have another problem – young people can be very conservative. 'We want to go on the mystery trip to Liverpool like last year – but then it won't be a mystery'. Maybe no one wants to make candles but they might once you start, and what have you lost by looking silly making candles on your own. Carol singing on your own is more problematic! If staff have a particular hobby or skill they can be encouraged to share it.

The programme should consist of activities and projects involving different timescales, short, medium and long-term (Riley, 2001). Myhill (1985) describes the idea of programme planning as a pyramid with long term planning for small numbers, perhaps a performance or expedition and the base being the short term activities that are available for everyone every time the club is open. Thus the annual camp would be at the top of the pyramid and a friendly hockey match half way down. Any good club will have a variety of activities planned at each level.

The coffee bar

Nearly every youth club has a coffee bar. Some simply sell sweets and drinks, others will provide a full meal and most involve young people in their running, wholly or partially. This is a good and usually sought after experience for young people in handling stock, counting money etc. However, I have never yet made a profit from a youth club coffee bar and they can take up a great deal of a club workers time going to buy stock, doing the accounts etc. Certainly it's a good idea to provide food, and these days the healthier the better. Cooking is a great activity to do with young people, giving opportunities for much conversation. Getting them to clean up afterwards is the hard bit!

Physical activity

With the current concern about obesity among young people – the number of obese young people doubled between 1993 and 2001 – (*Young People Now*, 5.2.03) youth clubs have a valuable role to play in encouraging physical activity that is fun, and different from school sports. Many youth clubs have access to a large hall or outside games area and can also arrange weekend outdoor activities. Games such as parachute games, or team games will keep even older adolescents engaged if they are fun.

The role of educator fits well with that of activity organiser, to ensure that activities are organised in order to educate, not as a substitute for it. However, this does mean thinking carefully about the type of activities that go on, especially in terms of meeting the needs of a wide variety of young people including those with disabilities and from different cultures. As Spence explains (1989), recreational, activity-based youth work is inherently biased towards a particular stereotyped conception of masculinity and being about cups, medals and physical prowess. Workers who noticed this tended to respond by introducing special activities for girls such as cooking, crafts, beauty, keep fit etc. (see Chapter 5). Where they still happen 'girl's nights', when activities like this are often put on to attract girls, may also include 'issue based group work' with them.

The workers

It also helps if workers are enjoying themselves. After all, in how many jobs would you be able to abseil or canoe or go to a pop concert, I even persuaded some young people to go and see Bob Dylan with me once! Youth work is not only a place where you can bring your own talents and enthusiasms and hopefully inspire others but also somewhere adults can learn new skills. Workers enthusiasm to have a go, at something like a modern dance or drama workshop, can introduce young people to new activities.

Getting out and about

This is the stuff that memories are made of. I am sure that if I bumped into one of my old members tomorrow, the conversation would be about the time I dragged them up Scafell Pike carrying tents, not the everyday life of the club. 'There is no good in a youth club that does only what is expected; high points are needed, new experiences' (Truman and Brent, 1995). For many young people youth club trips and holidays will have been their only holiday, 'the first time I had ever been on holiday for a whole week' (Rose, 1998). Day trips, even to quite nearby places, may not be something they would be able to do otherwise, and introduce young people to new experiences which they will remember for ever. For example, 'I knew we were going up a mountain but I didn't think it would be this big' (a young person on seeing Moel Famau) 'that's f-----ing steep!' (on seeing Sharp Edge). I am a big fan of mountains and have tried to instil some of my own enthusiasm into young people over the years, with varying degrees of success. 'Isn't it wonderfully peaceful and quiet up here?' 'It would be if you'd shut up!'

While a worker in Cheshire I often joined the Cheshire and Wirral Federations trips, run by their manager, Mike Stephenson. This was a good chance for young people from my club to meet those from other parts of the county. This is from one of Mike's evocative reports of a walk we did, which he used to send to all the young people involved afterwards:

> *What did it matter now that we had not been able to see the roof of Wales from Carnedd Llewelyn. It was enough now that we had planted our feet on those high places, that we had trod on the first snow of the winter, and that somehow we felt much closer together as a group of friends than when we started out.*

Many games and activities can be carried out in the outdoors other than the traditional, see Smith (1994) for creative ideas.

Trips don't have to be outdoors. Giving young people the experience of the theatre or ballet for the first time is easy to do, and is often an unforgettable experience for everyone. Subsidised tickets are often available. Young people are often unwilling to venture on to unknown territories and the youth club can help them to do so, just visiting another part of town may be a revelation for young people who would not have tried the journey alone. Giving young people access to the wider community and combatting social exclusion can be a powerful learning experience, Bradford (2004) cites a club visit to Northern Ireland.

Club holidays

The tradition of club holidays dates back to Stanley (1890) where girls were invited to stay in country houses; 'the happiness conferred is out of all proportion to the expense, to the trouble of the host'. It has been a long and valuable one which seems to be disappearing, and yet it is an extremely important part of club life. It is a great opportunity for young people to get away cheaply without their parents, but under some adult supervision, before they are able to go completely alone. There are still a large number of young people who do not get holidays away from home. Some clubs own their own activity centre which is an amazing asset to the work; it may range from a hut in a forest to a fully equipped residential centre, and can be used by the club regularly to get away for the weekend with groups of young people. These clubs are in a minority but it is always possible to find reasonable cheap accommodation or to camp. The tradition of camping still carried on so well by the Woodcraft Folk and Scouts and Guides gives young people an invaluable experience of learning to cope without hair dryers, and that there is life without computers and televisions. Being away from the responsibility of a building can also enable the youth worker to make better relationships with young people which can be maintained back at the club.

Many clubs have ventured overseas on youth exchanges, this needs a great deal of planning, and commitment from the young people, but there are organisations to help and the experience can be life changing.

Bureaucracy

It is increasingly important that youth workers are qualified to lead activities, and it is often easier to train a youth worker to teach rock climbing than to teach a rock climber to do youth work.

However, getting away from the club seems to have become more difficult as local authorities demand more and more forms, further in advance. It is ridiculous to be asked to supply the names and addresses of the young people going on a barge trip three months before the event or to have to get parental consent forms to take young people on a scavenger hunt in their local area. Risk assessment is obviously important, but what managers need to remember is that they have a trained and qualified work force, and asking a manager to check something already checked by a youth worker is overkill. Managers should be encouraging youth workers to undertake residentials by giving them time off in lieu, and paying part-time staff to go, instead of putting obstacles in their way. Many youth workers are not doing residentials because of the bureaucracy. Some will use this as an excuse not to organise them, but for many it is a real handicap. The loss of many 'in house' residential centres has not improved the position. Voluntary organisations and small voluntary clubs have more freedom to be spontaneous nowadays than the big clubs. Being able to be flexible in your programme can make the club an exciting place to be. 'If the weather is good we'll take the minibus and go to the nearest hill, or canal with the canoes', or 'why don't we ask club X if they fancy a pool competition?' If you have to ask permission a month before it won't happen.

Apart from a place to meet, the activities which youth clubs provide, such as the chance for young people to get away, have new experiences, enjoy the open air is an argument in itself. For example; in the early 1980s some money became available in my district to work with unemployed young people. We had a keen hill walking group at the club then who had often been on days out with us to the Lakes or Peak District and who wanted to go camping. They had no chance of affording to get away, so I asked my youth officer for the money. The reply came back that I had to write an application stating the educational benefits and it had to go to a committee etc. The weather was good and wouldn't be for long, and they wanted to go then. The momentum and enthusiasm for the project often can't wait, luckily my youth officer proved sympathetic.

Residentials

Residentials are a wonderful way of really getting to know a group, but it is a good idea to have formed relationships with the young people beforehand. It helps to draw up ground rules in advance that everyone agrees to. In my view the most important thing is that the staff get on well with each other, and have a similar attitude. If you can laugh about the police taking your minibus apart to look for stolen goods, perhaps not in front of them, and know that, at least in front of the young people you will receive support and backing, you have a valuable colleague. Due to the immense commitment required from staff, often without payment, it is important that they have a good time too – taking it in turns to stay up all night, or getting a couple of hours off at the pub can make a great deal of difference.

Residentials don't always have to be in cold windy spots involving mountains. Successful residentials involving sleeping on youth club floors can initiate young people into a whole new world of a different city, and allow them to meet other young people from different backgrounds.

Competitions

There is surely no worse sight than an adult screaming at a young person at a football match 'tackle him' or some such. While eventually acknowledging that if you enter you might as well do your best to win, I'm not convinced it's healthy. Borough or county wide events can work well for getting young people together to mix and have a good time; however, they also like to win. My brilliant idea of picking the teams by seeing who wanted to be in them always sank like a lead balloon. 'So you'd pick the England football team by asking who wants to play?'

Competitions are not always about sport, for example Gloucestershire Youth Service run a fashion show called 'Worn out Remade' making new clothes from old ones.

National and regional events run by UK Youth and the National Association of Clubs for Young People, such as an annual dance competition, football, snooker etc. can give a focus to the programme, and involve travel locally and even nationally. Taking part is the main thing; a local festival of youth had various categories including cookery. Unfortunately the boys' enthusiasm for baking scones waned at the sight of much fluffier ones, and ours became missiles on the return trip to the club in the minibus.

Internal club competitions are always a good standby for that evening when no-one really wants to do anything, especially if a fabulous prize is offered. Whacky ideas like Mission Impossible organised by Cheshire and Wirral Federation of Youth Clubs can involve the whole club in undertaking unusual tasks, and a successful way of involving youth and adult groups was a community general quiz organised with groups of users against each other.

Issues

In the 1980s there was something in youth work called the 'hidden curriculum'. This meant that, although young people thought they were coming in to the club to meet their mates, catch up on the gossip and have a game of pool, in fact they were going to be educated and have their awareness of issues raised. There was a time in the 1980s when youth work seemed only to be about issues, making sure that young people took them on board. However, as Jeffs and Smith (1989) have argued, there was no clear definition of what the work represented and what it sought to achieve. There was a great deal of training about issues, about sexism, racism, disability awareness and hetero-sexism. Much of this training was good and led to improved awareness by staff, and hopefully better practice. However, while raising consciousness, much of it did not really help workers to change their practice. There was often a distinct lack of management enthusiasm and support for the training, and an inability to help workers to put it into practice. Issue based work, of course, cannot happen in a vacuum. Young people need to have fun at a youth club, and while undertaking activities, otherwise they won't come. This may seem self evident, but the concentration on education in quite a narrow sense has led some youth clubs to over emphasise formal approaches to discussion, so that a course will be put on and young people engage in a programme. Obviously if this idea comes from the young people it's great, but there are other ways of tackling subjects informally, and young people are often more likely to open up while engaged in an activity, this is one of the reasons I like hill walking so much.

Too much concentration on issues can make young people feel they are in school and 'being taught'. It is also often difficult to introduce an issues session into an open youth club. It's a bit like trying to talk politics in the Labour Club while the bingo is on. Although workers know that part of their job is to raise awareness, the young people may think they have come in to play pool. This does not mean of course that young people should be left to get on with it and not challenged about their behaviour. In fact the best time to discuss issues is when they happen. 'Why is a racist joke inappropriate? Why is it not a true statement that you would get a job if all the immigrants were sent home? Why should we spend the clubs resources to make it more accessible for people with disabilities? Why should everyone get a turn on the pool table – even if they aren't very good?' Using questions as a start in conversations can get issues discussed.

The youth club can provide an ideal environment for discussing issues with young people, but it is important that they choose the issues that matter to them. If the subject of drugs is already being discussed in the club it's much more likely that young people will respond positively to the idea of inviting the local drugs worker along to talk about their work. Issues such as healthy eating are important to young people and clubs can make a real difference, for instance, the Cwmbran Centre in Wales recently won an award for promoting healthy eating. They provided cooking classes, an allotment scheme and a café. Global youth work is an important concept which can be introduced into youth club programmes, young people these days are increasingly concerned about environmental and developmental issues, and youth club workers can enable young people to see links between their own lives and needs and those of the rest of the world (Bourn, 2003).

Residential experiences also provide opportunities for getting to terms with issues such as drinking and safe sex. It is important that ground rules are discussed beforehand but of course sneaking into each others rooms is as much part of the fun as is smuggling in the booze. It's also important that workers agree together how to approach issues which could potentially be difficult, whether it is OK to let older young people drink a few cans for example.

National initiatives

Government policy over the years has recognised the potential of youth work to work on educational issues and help in national initiatives. A 1995 White Paper, *Tackling Drugs Together*, highlighted the contribution that could be made by youth workers, usually as part of a wider campaign to promote good health. From 1990 a special section was introduced in *Young People Now* on health issues (Davies, 1999) and many projects and clubs had their work publicised there. Other professionals became interested in youth workers ability to engage with young people around health issues (Robertson, 2000). The rise of AIDS from the late 1980s brought some new funding to the youth service, usually in the form of detached or street workers.

Discipline and control

This is the tricky one of course, and probably the reason that many workers don't like club work. The use of a building causes such problems. Many of the buildings designed as youth clubs, and many that were not, are just impossible to use properly with the number of staff available unless young people are able to respect the club and each other. The key thing here is relationships; young people who are not treated with respect will not give it back. One of the main issues that youth clubs have in terms of behaviour is that many of the young people who use them are very angry. They are angry not with us as workers but with themselves and their lives. The most important thing is that we are non-judgemental; meaning that we do not make pre-judgements and are concerned to react to the behaviour and not the person. We are accepting of the whole person and interested enough in them to find out what makes them behave like that. Maybe a youth worker is the first adult to be really interested in the views of a young person. It does not mean that there are no boundaries, in fact young people will establish these fairly quickly and like to know they are there, but they may be different boundaries. For example, should we be too concerned about the language used by young people among themselves? It is important not to make rules that are bound to be broken. A dichotomy between youth workers approval and disapproval of members' behaviour has always existed, for instance Bunt and Gargrave (1980) found that some workers 'instead of seeking to attract the 'young savages' and the 'rougher classes' whose behaviour runs counter to social norms, excluded them from their clubs'.

Williamson (1997) suggests that while youth work provides social gathering places, there is pressure to present a good image, which is best achieved by getting rid of the trouble makers. My research suggests that these are often the same young people who have been excluded from school, or have excluded themselves (Robertson, 1999 and Chapter 8).

Banning never really seems to work. If many of the young people barred from the youth club are also being excluded from school, surely these are the young people we should be working with not throwing out on the streets. It is always important to remember that young people who attend choose to do so. Early in my career, I became wary of the sanction after a young man I had banned from the centre was beaten with a leather belt by his father because of it.

In Phil Cohen's (1997) seminal work he looks at issues of territoriality and discourse among young people and how the 'Growing Up 'game is played out. He imagines a scenario of a male middle class teacher or youth worker with a progressive outlook confronting a group of lads. The youth worker tries to establish a non-authoritarian relationship, using common interests or similarities such as football or clothes. However, the lads are trying to elicit expressions of difference as a function of the workers position, making jokes about him. The workers options, according to Cohen, are either to turn the cheek, in which case they will probably assign him to a residual category, not friend or enemy but mug! And the insults may get worse. Or he can stand on his dignity and assert authority with threats or punishment, in which case the lads have won because they have located him as an enemy. This is a common experience for youth workers, the problem is knowing at what level to respond. If they play along then they have 'lost control', if they crack down the young people may accuse them of mis-reading the situation – 'we were only having a laugh' and they have lost the chance of making the type of relationship they want. It's a difficult game to play and the only way to succeed really is to relate to each other properly and not hide behind the expected behaviours. Young people are used to playing this game and it's confusing for them when we refuse to play it and react in a different way to their behaviour.

Cohen (1997) interestingly, suggests that the process by which local authorities provide facilities is incomprehensible to their eventual user, i.e.

young people. 'It is something they do for us. But if these facilities are mysteriously 'given' kids are well aware that they have not been made a present of them' (p79). However, as the organisers want members, not just passive consumers, they construct members committees etc. As the club is in a catchment area, rival groups may struggle to assert control but also, and more interestingly for our purposes, they trigger behaviour designed to test whether these facilities really do belong to their members, so that waves of petty vandalism ensue and boredom is killed! 'It's our club so we can do what we like'. Only by young people having a real ownership will this problem be solved, but ownership by which group and on whose terms? Cohen's work gives a fascinating insight into what are commonly experienced behaviours, and the ways in which young people control what happens; but in a way that is ultimately unhelpful to them, as perhaps the club will be closed, or they will get barred. There must be a way found to work alongside young people and not against them. Because you need to be consistent it's best not to have too many rules, and not to make the major threat too soon. If exclusion for a calming down period is your last resort, don't use it too early.

Discipline is often seen as a masculine thing; you need to be a big man to control the boys. The point is that ultimately we are aiming for self-control, and for the young people to work together in such a way that there is no need for obvious 'discipline'. The taunt of 'you can't control us' is bound to be true, physically if young people want to throw their weight around they are very difficult to stop. I was very proud of myself one night after an extended discussion with a group on the theme of, it's time to go home now, we've all got beds to go to etc. when they suddenly left. I turned round in triumph only to realise my burly co-worker had walked in and my triumph was short lived. Spence (1989) makes the point that male workers will often fail to recognise the value of more subtle and diversionary tactics, but sometimes a big growly voice is very helpful!

Above all, as Truman and Brent (1995) emphasise we need to remember that, 'troublemaking is a phase with a lot of kids – you have to make clear what the choices are, perhaps they will remember and consider'.

Another useful tool is a contract with members. This can work well if introduced properly and arrived at in a fully participative fashion with members. They then know clearly what the ground rules are and accept them. Castlemilk Youth Centre in Glasgow operates this system and this ensures the young people have a sense of ownership of the club.

Membership

From the early years of youth clubs, a membership system was normal practice – it probably comes from the origins of the idea of clubs (see Chapter

2) and many clubs still continue it. The idea is to make young people feel a sense of ownership and involvement in 'their' club. Sometimes membership is compulsory after a couple of visits and will mean that young people's names and addresses are taken and there may be a fee involved. The National associations ask for numbers of members for insurance purposes, but many clubs do not have a strict system and any young person of the right age will be admitted. Names should still be taken though – its one of the ways after all of starting to engage young people in conversation. Clubs have sometimes used the idea of membership to restrict attendance to a certain catchment area, or to control numbers, but it is important not to end up excluding young people. If young people are prepared to travel across town to a club it seems to me they should be welcomed. Young people can be notoriously territorial, and we should be about breaking down barriers not creating them. However, now that young people often travel long distances to school the idea of their local club may not be so relevant, as they may well want to go to the club near their friend's house instead.

Democracy and participation

The environment inside a club can be viewed as a microcosm of a local community. Democracy and involvement is dependent on people overcoming the problems that arise in getting a consensus, and from the tendency of the most powerful to get their ideas taken on board. The way that youth club workers use their power and authority in the youth club is a model for young people in their own dealings with others.

The idea that the young people themselves should be involved in running their own club existed in the early days. Stanley (1890) recommended that the girls have a means of cheap refreshment and that they run this themselves. The coffee bar has long been an institution in clubs, and can be successfully run by the members, but it is never going to make much money. Stanley established girls' committees but felt that you could not expect to start a club with members fit to take a responsible part in the management. The girls' committee would need looking after and supporting for some time and need overseeing.

Evans (1965) points to a significant change in the organisation of youth clubs in the 1930s with a growing concern to offer young people opportunities to run their own clubs: both for building self respect and self confidence and in enabling club programmes to be built around their interests. Real efforts were made to encourage young people to express their opinions and act on them. Most of these young people were older than those using clubs nowadays, and at work. In 1939 only 13% of young people continued in education after the statutory school leaving age of 14, and only 4% after 16.

In 1927 Brew wrote one of the first books about how to run a club. It was the first statement of modern youth work (Smith, 2000) and was concerned with the making of good citizens, and self-government in the club was part of it. 'The club at its best creates a society of personalities with a community sense – the essence of good citizenship.' She thought club committees were important to give everyone a chance to contribute to the life of the group.

Prior to the Second World War, young people played a significant role in the organisation of clubs (Smith, 1988). During the war this situation was probably strengthened by the shortage of adult leaders and the numbers of senior members who were called up. The club was seen as important in the training of citizenship. Much greater responsibility for the running of clubs was given to senior members and senior member training schemes were set up at local, regional and national levels.

In 1942 the report on the Youth Advisory Council recommended representation from young people. The Albermarle report (Ministry of Education,1960) highlighted the role of young people in running the service as the fourth partner giving self-programming special prominence (Davies, 1999), although no attempt was made to give young people a place on the Youth Service Development Council formed following the Albermarle Report. In the Withywood Experiment the newly built youth club was largely run by its members (Sharpe, 2004).

Milson-Fairbairn (DES, 1969) wanted young people to be 'active citizens' and the Thompson Report (1982) strongly endorsed participation and political education. Much youth work rhetoric concerns participation but there is a contradiction in this, as Spence (1989) points out, in that the services aims are based on helping young people develop into an adult idea of maturity. Participation in the youth club is generally concerned with building up the ability of the young people to do things such as organise the classic ice skating trip (Smith, 1980). Actually, in many ways, we are underselling young people's skills to say they can't organise things. The main problem is that if there is an adult around to do it, particularly a paid adult, many feel why should they get involved. However, if there is an assumption in the club that small groups will be working together on different projects, one of which might be a trip away, this can work well and will give young people new skills and build on existing ones. Smith's (1980) example demonstrates the importance of process – there are many activities which young people may start and complete, but not repeat! A newsletter is a common one (there must have been hundreds of first issues of club newspapers), but even so the young people get a lot out of the experience. Workers are often wary of trying something again if it 'didn't work last time', but if this is a different group of young people (and even if it's the same ones!) who want to put a pantomime on then they need encouragement.

However, it can be important sometimes for an adult to ensure that an event happens. I worked with a group of young disabled people once to produce a piece of drama. The Head of Service had decreed that every youth group would produce something on the theme of empowerment to be showcased in the town hall. Keeping my small group together was difficult, as was encouraging them to do something which needed a great deal of self-confidence. It was my responsibility, I felt, to ensure they did it. They had already learnt a good deal about working together and expressing their ideas but it was the actual production that meant the most.

Administration

In some clubs young people have been able to become very involved in the day-to-day running of the club, handling money etc., and there is no reason why this shouldn't happen. The issue was a real one for Bunt and Gargrave (1980) who felt that youth workers needed to do much better in terms of relinquishing power to young people. Not much has changed since their day but part of the problem must be that young people get older. The usual time of involvement for a young person in the day-to-day life of a youth club is usually not more than three years and they are the years when a great deal of other things are happening for young people, sex, drugs and exams for example. Young people inevitably operate to shorter timescales than adults, and therefore may be reluctant to make long term commitments.

Rules

If young people are involved in the club with an active members' committee and meetings that make rules you will often find they will be far stricter than a youth worker. One members' committee ended up banning so many members that they formed a non-members' committee to try and wrest power back! Young people becoming empowered in this way can also lead to them making decisions which may not be in the interest of the club as a whole. Particularly on equal opportunities issues, members' committees need clear guidelines.

Wider forums

Increasingly throughout the 1990s young people were being asked to participate in local youth forums. The 1998 Youth Service Audit (NYA) showed that over 60 per cent of local authorities had or planned to have youth forums with financial backing from a wide range of sources such as Single Regeneration Budgets. There is now a UK Youth Parliament and many other participatory projects around the country and three quarters of service plans (Merton et al., 2005) indicate this is now being taken on board. If youth club members are to have the confidence to engage at this level, then the club will often need to help them, otherwise it may be only those young people who are already participating confidently at school who get involved. Elected committees are a feature of many clubs in addition to the adults co-opted on to the adult management committee. To get ideas from the whole club or to talk over an issue which has occurred, it is very useful to get into the habit of general meetings, where all members and staff of the club can attend and voice their concerns. These can be reasonably informal as long as everyone gets a chance to have their say.

The Impact of Youth Work research (DfES, 2005) found that young people's participation in the running of their facilities was central to practice in most youth services studied.

The local Youth Associations can provide valuable initiatives for getting young people involved in decision making including the Youth Parliament. The National Association of Clubs for Young People recently launched the Power Up Project to conduct research into young people's views on decision making.

Peer education

Another form of participation, peer education, has also grown rapidly in the 1990s with resources being made available to work with young people on projects such as sex education, where young people visit schools or youth clubs often performing a piece of drama or engaging young people in discussion. This type of initiative, working with a small group of young people, can really benefit the members of that group, as well as those they educate, helping them to grow in self-confidence and knowledge.

Connexions has been concerned to get the views of young people from the outset, which should be a good thing in the development of a new service but Smith (2002) sounds a note of caution as he feels the fine words about young people having a voice are really about the feedback they can give as consumers – they are not making decisions.

Stories about clubs

Of course there was 'Byker Grove' on TV, and a famous film of the 1950s made by Karl Reisz. *We are the Lambeth Boys* was set in a youth club, but to get a really good picture of what goes on in a club you have to get involved. However, there are some good accounts to read of youth clubs at various points in their history which still speak to us today. *Touching Lives* (Rose, 1998) is a good example, a fascinating account of a Jewish club showing the value of volunteering, support, leadership and involving many different activities. Above all it shows the value of commitment – founder members of the club moved to being workers and members of the management committee. Judaism was at the core of this club where young people learnt to love and respect their religion.

Another Jewish youth worker, Henriques, ran a boy's club in East London and wrote about his experiences. *Club Leadership* (1933, revised ed., 1951) is written in a dogmatic style , explaining the need for clubs for the formation of character and the use of activities such as camping to develop every side of their nature. Jeffs has written about Henriques in *Basil Henriques and The House of Friendship* (Jeffs, 2004) describing the influence he had.

Mary Blandy describes a very different kind of club in *Razors Edge* (Blandy, 1967). Her title is taken from the Albermarle Report which said that 'youth work requires a tense day-to-day walking on a razor edge between sympathy and surrender'. She describes the young people as 'unclubbables', and the club set up for them had a constant struggle to obtain premises and funding. What really comes across in her book is how much she got out of the work, and how much she enjoyed being with the young people. If there is a central message about good practice in youth clubs Blandy demonstrates it with her enthusiasm for the work and her concern for the young people she works with. Her stories are extremely amusing and describe situations which still occur in clubs; above all her club was fun and that is why young people came and why she worked there. Generating a 'fun' atmosphere in the club should be the central task of the youth club worker: if you stop enjoying it give up! Ray Sharpe (2004) describes the club at Withywood where he was the first full-time leader and fresh from the National College, was determined that the young people should run the club.

In *Angry Adolescents* a teacher of youth workers (Goldman, 1969) describes the setting up of a club in a village hall on a new estate in the 1960s. He and his wife were concerned about the lack of facilities for young people, and the fact that they were seen as a 'problem'. However, the young people were initially hostile and suspicious and thought the youth workers must be making money out of it. Why else would they run a club? I had that reaction 30 years later in my village too!

Also from the 1960s, Spencer et al.'s 1964 book *Stress and Release in an Urban Estate* devotes two chapters to a direct account of youth club work, and a more modern example, *Alive and Kicking* (Truman and Brent, 1995) describes the same club in Bristol and what it did and continues to do for young people; 'their vision was expanding, their view of the world changing, finding out there were other ways to be' (p33). They too emphasise that 'you have to love the work, I was never bored'.

Chapter 5

Equal Opportunities

The youth club should of course be a refuge from the real world, a place where everyone is valued equally and treated with respect. However, clubs often seem to be a microcosm of the real world where people are discriminated against and abused. This chapter examines issues of equal opportunities in youth clubs covering class, gender, black young people, disabled young people and lesbian and gay young people. There are many other groups of young people that the youth service and youth clubs work with and who can be encouraged to attend youth clubs, such as young refugees and asylum seekers, children from travelling communities, young people in care.

Young people are subject to ageism as a group and it is important that the youth club is one place where they are treated respectfully and where their views are taken into account. Most youth clubs have age restrictions and it is important they are enforced fairly – adolescents need space on their own but clubs should also look to provide times when those under 14 can meet together. This is often impossible in a one night a week club or village club and then it is probably sensible to have a younger age limit in view of the smaller number of young people potentially attending. Junior clubs for those under the usual youth club 'senior' night age deserve more support than they get from youth service resources. Often there is no local authority funding for these clubs but they are invaluable in beginning to make relationships with young people and can provide valuable opportunities for 'senior' youth club members to get involved in helping.

Apart from age restrictions, most youth clubs have maintained an open door policy on senior nights and built separate provision for disabled young people, gay young people, girls, young men, or young black people into the programme when they have been motivated to do so, as resources have allowed, or management pressure has dictated. The Thompson Report (1982) gave particular emphasis to so called 'targeted work' and led to the development of many specialist projects for these groups. However, these were, and indeed still continue to be, resourced in a haphazard and often short term fashion.

Thompson et al. (1982) found that the ratio of men to women in full-time posts was 3:1 and 10:1 for officers. This contrasted starkly with the part-time workforce which depended heavily upon women. In the 1980s, as 'girls work' made its presence felt in the service, specialist 'girls workers' began to be appointed, sometimes on a county or borough basis. The problem with this was that the agenda of the management team, and of many male club workers, was that if this girl's work was a necessary evil it would be marginalised and quietly disposed of when resources got tight.

The passing of Section 28 of the Local Government Act of 1988 allowed managers not only to refuse to fund openly gay provision, on the grounds that it was against the law, but also made them suspicious of single sex work.

The same type of thing happened with work with young people with disabilities and here managers had the excuse that there were not sufficient disabled staff around to be recruited.

By and large, however, youth services adopted equal opportunities statements and policies, some more inclusive than others; Croydon's Tory council refused to include sexual orientation in 1992, for example. Equal opportunities training, around issues of gender, race, disability and sometimes hetero-sexism, was made mandatory for full-time workers in many Local Authorities throughout the 1980s and into the 1990s. Money for training received a boost in the 1980s with the LEA Training Grants Scheme which ear marked funds for full and part-time worker training.

However, the days of women's committees and positive action were short lived and never arrived in the rural shire counties, where it was felt by many that there was no problem with racism in counties where there were no black people.

Female and black workers often felt marginalised and unsupported and went about organising support for themselves, meeting nationally and locally. At the first ministerial conference in 1989 there were only 12 black participants out of 250 (Davies, 1999). This lack of women managers, especially black ones, continues today.

Equal opportunities is about more than finding a label for a young person, it is about valuing all young people and treating them according to their needs. Not all young people want the same attention from you as a worker, but they all have a right to your time and it is important to ensure everyone has equal opportunity, to go on trips, to join events and to attend the club. It is therefore important to think about the staff who work in the club and to provide a variety of approachable adults for the young people to relate to. The variety, cost and timing of the activities needs careful consideration, so that young people are not discriminated against or excluded: for example not all young people enjoy sport.

Staff training in equal opportunities is vital and it needs to be part of all youth work training but the important thing for staff is experience. Much discrimination and stereotyping comes from fear of the unknown and once workers start to extend their practice, with black young people, young people with disabilities, gay young people, and find that their youth work skills in making relationships with young people hold good, they find the work rewarding as well as challenging.

It is important that young people who use the club are aware of its policies on equal opportunities and aware that discriminatory language and attitudes are not acceptable. When young people are involved in decision making they need to be bound by these policies too, so that a particular group cannot vote to exclude another as it would be against club policy. It is not enough simply to open doors, many young people may be isolated in the community and need outreach work, through schools or care homes for example, to be informed of the club and some may need help to get there, company or transport. A report by the Social Exclusion Unit on young people in care (www.socialexclusionunit.gov.uk) found that out-of-school activities were essential for raising self-esteem and confidence, enhancing social skills, increasing motivation towards education and encouraging independence. Also presumably for having fun.

Class and the 'unclubbables'

Historically, youth clubs were created primarily for the use of working class boys and girls and have been funded and built in areas of poverty and deprivation. However, Jephcott's research of 1954 (Osgerby, 1998) found that there was a tendency for clubs to draw membership primarily from the more respectable sections of the working and lower middle class rather than the 'below average' child from the 'below average home'. Generally the idea of Albermarle (Ministry of Education, 1960) was to provide for working girls and boys the type of provision that was available to students in universities. Clubs were built in many of the new estates constructed in the 1960s, but, of course, with demographic change clubs can end up in a different type of community from that originally envisaged.

DES research of the 1980s (DES, 1983) found that almost two times as many C2/Ds and Es had attended youth clubs than AB and C1s and this was still the case in the DES survey of 1995. It was more overcrowded at home for working class young people, and middle class young people tended to fuse their school and leisure lives (Jeffs and Smith, 1989).

Are there some young people who we won't be able to get involved in a youth club? Such as the 'unclubbables': 'the seriously disorganised', 'the disaffected', 'the unattached' and 'the socially excluded'. The language has changed over the years, but debates about how to work with those groups of young people seen as 'trouble makers' by their communities has been a constant youth service theme. Arguments about whether the service should be working in a targeted way with young offenders came to a head with the introduction of 'intermediate treatment' following the 1969 Children and Young Person Act. Participation in these schemes was seen by many workers to be against the principle of 'voluntary attendance' that is one of the key principles of youth work. These arguments were also raised when youth workers participated in Youth Training Schemes and the Community Programme in the 1980s, and more recently, Youth Offending Teams and Connexions. Generally managers of youth services have been quick to lose their principles when money is on offer from the government. The Community and Youth Workers Union maintained a principled stand against the Community Programme in the 1980s, but generally it has been up to individual workers to decide how much they want to be involved in these types of schemes, albeit heavily influenced by management.

There was a huge increase in unemployment among young people and a widening gap between rich and poor in the 1980s and 1990s. The images of affluent young people which had influenced the Albermarle Report were replaced by those of mass unemployment and despair. However, there was no particular focus on the issue of the different class backgrounds of youth club attenders/non-attenders (Davies, 1999). Davies feels an opportunity was lost for work on personal identity and collective action which could have complemented that being done on issues of race and gender.

By the 1990s government initiatives on crime reduction involving the youth service, such as the Youth Action Scheme meant that the youth service was being asked to target working class young men, 67 per cent of those worked with were male (France and Wiles, 1997). This often was seen to involve providing diversionary activities to 'keep them off the streets'. The theme has always been the containment of working class young people rather than seizing the opportunity to help them to reflect on their lives, for example. Youth work nowadays, and under the Transforming Youth Work and Connexions agendas, is being increasingly targeted at poor areas, and this means that middle class kids miss out on the benefits of youth work. Youth clubs can provide much needed support for all young people and the opportunity to meet and mix with a variety of other young people and increase their social networks.

Work with girls

Although the first National Organisation for Clubs was that established in 1911 for girls clubs, they had in fact existed since 1861 (Steward, 2001). Stanley (1890), one of the early pioneers of girls work, suggested that work with girls was about 'helping them find out their own powers and raise them more in their own estimation'. The National Organisation worked alongside young women and campaigned for better conditions in factories, for example. However, by 1949 the distinctive focus of the work had changed from helping working girls with issues, to leisure activities (Turnbull, 2001). In 1953, for example, the National Association of Girls and Mixed Clubs as it was then known, recommended to club leaders that they arrange 'girls interest groups' within their club programmes: suggested topics were 'planning a wedding, planning a children's party and washing and ironing!'

Mixed clubs

The National Organisation for Girls Clubs merger with mixed clubs, plus the 1950s back to the home movement, led to a take over by the boys. There was support for mixed clubs from Brew who felt that 'boys and girls brought different gifts to the enrichment of club life'. She felt there was a case for some separate provision within a context of mixed provision (Smith, 2001). However, this rise in mixed clubs led to the demise of girls' clubs, and by 1963 only 216 girls clubs survived as opposed to nearly 2,000 boys' clubs. The Albermarle Report (Ministry of Education, 1960) emphasised the value of mixed activities, but concluded that 'fewer girls than boys are members of youth organisations and much thought will need to be given to ways of attracting them, and studies made of their particular needs'. Girls were often seen as 'an activity for the boys' as an 'extra' or as a 'problem': the lack of women workers compounded this situation:

> *If youth clubs are to offer a really helpful service to girls, there must be an increase of women in the service . . . The woman youth leader is . . . frequently expected to run the girls part very much as the poor relation of the boys.*
>
> (Hamner, 1964, quoted by Davies, 1999)

According to Davies (1999) girls work at the end of the 1960s was essentially reactive and insufficiently inventive. The National Association of Youth Clubs, having dropped girls from its title in 1961, became a major advocate of mixed clubs while the National Association of Boys' Clubs, which maintained that title until very recently, championed the right of boys to meet separately. The boys' club movement has always been able to attract powerful support from influential 'old boys' and to raise money from them. It also had a clear philosophy about the need for separate provision, which was not articulated for girls until the 1970s, by which time there were major cuts in resources. A survey done for Milson-Fairburn (DES, 1969) showed that girls made up less than a third of club membership.

By 1975 women workers had begun to radically analyse their youth work, and to argue for male-free space for girls to develop their own identities. Women workers support groups formed and workers put on girls only activities such as the 1977 NAYC initiative 'Boys Rule Not OK' offering girls non-traditional activities such as outdoor work. These initiatives caused enormous opposition at ground level, not just from the boys but also from male workers and managers. For example, the London Union of Youth Clubs sacked its field officer for encouraging separate work with young women.

In the 1980s, books such as *Coming in from the Margins* (Carpenter and Young, 1986) and events such as the national Working with Girls conferences, and especially the establishment of the girls' work unit at the NAYC, inspired a generation of female youth workers who were trying to reconcile their feminist beliefs with their youth work practice. I returned from these conferences motivated and enthusiastic about starting girls only activities, despite lack of male management support. Writers like Dale Spender (1980) pointed out the domination of schooling by boys, and I realised that boys were able to claim most of my attention by their behaviour. Girls' nights which would allow female staff to spend time with the girls in a safe and undisrupted club became usual; even in outposts like Devon. In London and other major cities, specific full-time girls' work posts were created. However, the girls work cause was not helped by the Thompson Report of 1982 which gave only lukewarm endorsement to separate provision. HMI reports in the 1980s did highlight the lack of funding for work with young women in most local authorities (Davies, 1999). In 1987 women workers throughout the country were appalled at the closure of the NAYC girls work unit, although the National Organisation for Work with Girls and Young Women continued until 1994. The demise of ILEA in 1990 was a blow to youth work generally, and especially to girls work, and helped develop a situation where the work could be picked off as 'trendy lefty' by those wanting to keep the resources for what they called 'mainstream' i.e. boys work. Today it seems that to some extent little progress has been made. The idea of 'girls only' space in clubs is still often greeted with a great deal of opposition and confrontation both from staff and management, and from the young people themselves. The pressure in youth work to 'keep them off the streets' is largely of course about keeping young men off the streets as they are seen as disruptive, dangerous and potentially criminal. Therefore the emphasis in club work has been on boys and those methods of work which will prove most attractive to them (Spence, 1989).

A NACYS report of 1988 found that girls work was regarded with mistrust in the service and this is often still the case. Where girls' work is done today, it is usually because of the commitment of individual women workers often up against a lack of support from male workers – if not, indeed, outright opposition. The same arguments that I felt had been won in the 1980s still resurface, for example when students are on placement trying to institute some girls work. The lack of women officers to support the work has not helped, but all too often women become afraid to stand up for the work when resources are tight and numbers of girls involved are small. Male workers will often cynically opt for a girl's night to have a night off. They should not be involved in the actual provision, but need to offer the support and supervision that the part-time women workers often running the programme really need.

Coming at a time of cuts in resources it could be argued that girls' work, and particularly the idea of girls' nights in youth clubs, was not supportive of the youth club ethos of mixed clubs. The problem was that separate work was often not done with the boys who gathered outside on girls' nights and understandably were annoyed at losing a club night while a small number of girls were allowed in. The boys ended up being the victims of this approach and perhaps it was too much to expect that they would learn about their sexism from this approach. Even if there were boys' nights as well, once the club became closed to different groups on different nights there was less provision, and young people had to go somewhere else on that night. In Withywood in 1997 for example there was one open mixed night for seniors, one for inters, and a reasonably well attended girls' night, average 27. Which in my experience was a high attendance for girls' nights, based as they often were on small group work around issues.

Attendance

Boys' work has dominated the provision, not only by the types of activities provided, but also numerically. In the 1960s, while suggesting that girls only really came to clubs to meet boys, a London Federation of Boys' Clubs report concluded that girls needed separate space in the clubs. Macalister Brew also suggested that mixed clubs attracted more boys than girls (Davies, 1999). In 1983 a report concluded that users of clubs were 'essentially young, male and C2/D/E' (DES, 1983: 44). Of those currently attending youth clubs in the survey 46 per cent were female (DES, 1983: 37). Smith (1988) found considerable evidence that this figure overstated their usage, and in fact it was only in the under 12s that girls made up this proportion. In the 1995 survey into participation in the youth service (DES, 1995), boys' participation was higher than girls' for all age groups.

It is still true today that youth clubs are not only dominated numerically by boys, as shown by Ofsted reports and LEA surveys, but that the space within them is also male dominated and the activities often have a distinctly male bias. Ofsted reports today still highlight the fact that in many authorities attendance of young women is a concern e.g. Somerset Ofsted Report 2002 'Attendance by young women was low, representing less than 38 per cent of all young people involved, significantly less than the 48 per cent figure supplied by the service'. Research has shown (Holden, 1989) that girls normally attend clubs with other girl friends. Friendship with a small group of close girl friends is very important for adolescent girls, and the main activity at the club is chatting to their friends.

'Girls' activities'

In the new buildings of the 1960s separate space for girls was planned:

> *. . . in the successful club girls will make full use of the facilities for practical and physical activities as well as being attracted by the social side of club life. There is, however, a strong case for providing them with something extra in the form of a beauty parlour or powder room.*
>
> (Ministry of Education Building Bulletin 22, 1963: 31)

This was en suite with a carpeted sitting room area. These powder rooms still exist in many buildings, often with large mirrors useful for dance or keep fit. Carpenter and Young (1986) suggest that Albermarle reinforced the stereotyping of leisure activities with large halls being built for the boys, and the girls confined to the coffee bar or toilets. The allocation of the toilets to young women to use as 'their' locale left the relative power of the young men unchallenged (Smith, 1994).

Often, it is difficult for girls to join in club activities. Unwritten rules in clubs such as 'winner stays on the pool table' often make it impossible for the girls to play together or to join in at all. Sometimes an older, inferior table is set aside for the girls! (Holden, 1989). In Holden's research, she found that young women did not take part in what were seen as 'boys' activities' such as football, table tennis and weight training. These activities were often prioritised in the club, and money spent on football kit and so on.

The idea that girls need particular activities is still prevalent, but a club which provides a well rounded programme should be able to include both sexes in most activities. The use of 'girls' activities such as sewing, cooking or craft work are often done to encourage conversation. Sitting down having conversations is something that should also be planned for the boys if workers are to build relationships with them and engage in informal education. Conversely, girls often get a great deal out of traditionally 'male' outdoor activities such as rock climbing, hill walking or canoeing, which involve working together in small groups and developing trust. One of my proudest moments in youth work was seeing one of the girls from my club leap between the rocks known as Adam and Eve on the top of Tryffen in Wales. I had told the group about them and that the idea is to leap from one to the other, something I was too scared to attempt myself. As we reached the summit Lynda went straight away and did the leap. There were a crowd of young men sitting about and nerving themselves up to do it!

Encouraging girls to try new activities, and offering both them and the boys role models of women, not only partaking in activities, but leading them, is important. In the same way, male workers should be engaging in such traditional 'girls' activities as dance and art.

Access

Access to premises is important, and the timing of the club, needs to be sensitive to parental concerns about their daughters being out late at night. The girl's night could meet earlier or transport home could be offered. Many clubs working with Asian girls have been able to arrange this or to open at the weekends. Well lit access is fundamental. Girls do not want to have to walk down a dark alley to the club, even in a group, and we should not expect them to.

Sexism

In 1989 Holden found that, despite over ten years of 'girls work', mixed provision was still inherently sexist. The sad thing is that in the 21st century this is still the case. The new youth service agenda of combating disaffection is still largely targeted at boys; girls only really get a mention in the context of preventing. As Steward (2001) suggests, in the context of current policy, disaffection means that young women still rarely have a high profile in the work. Osgerby (1998) contends that as girls are perceived as much less of a threat to public order than boys, they have remained marginal to the institutions of state and voluntary youth provision. When the service has targeted young people who offend and created specialist projects for them, it was, and still is in reality, targeting young men. Batsleer (1996) feels that the work nowadays is closer in spirit to the very conservative agenda of the 1890s than to the more recent past encompassing, as it does, ideas of 'protection' and 'dependency'. The early initiatives and commitment to self-activity and self-discipline have not been strong enough to prevent this agenda from re-emerging.

At the beginning of youth work, when girls' work was at the forefront, many girls' clubs were run by well educated middle class women. The individuals involved brought a radical edge to the work and were often involved in a variety of reformist movements. As such they created a curriculum which attempted to raise the girls' awareness in order to improve their social situation.

The next important time for girls' work was in the 1970s and 1980s, when workers discovered feminism and brought it into the clubs. Feminism now is often derided, and many young women do not want to be identified with its media stereotype of stridency and dungarees. The girls' work banner seems rather low now but there is no excuse for youth clubs to treat a portion of their membership as second class.

Work with boys

In many clubs, as suggested above, youth work tends to focus on work with boys, with their needs such as space to kick a ball predominating. There is also still a thriving boys' club movement and many clubs still go under the name of Boys' Club even when they are mixed. In the early 1990s I was sent an outraged memo by an education officer who had suddenly realised there were such things:

> *I am alarmed at this being the . . . Boys Club. Do they take girls? If so, would you please change the name, e.g. to . . . Youth Club. If not, please withhold any further payments until we have sorted this out.*

Easier said than done! Boys' clubs are often well supported and good at raising funds from the 'old boys', and so consider it important to keep the name, and many are not reliant on the local authority for funding and own their premises.

Specific work with boys on issues of sexism was developed during the 1980s mainly as a response to the rise of girls work (Lloyd, 1985) but while a girls' night in many places became an accepted part of the club, the provision of single gender work with boys, and the staff to do it, is rare. The clubs need to change the macho culture that often dominates them. Until that happens it will be difficult to do 'boys' work' in small groups around issues that concern them, in the way that is possible in 'girls' work'. Clubs need to look hard at their programme, develop more truly mixed activities, make it a condition of residentials that they are mixed, and that the boys do their share of the work. Boys-only provision still exists in boys' clubs, but these settings are rarely used to get young men to look at their attitudes or behaviour and often rather encourage the traditional activities such as football and boxing. Singh Gill (2001) suggests that boys work at the moment has more to do with the enforcement of power and control than creating an understanding of masculinity and sexism. He feels that boys' work needs to build a bridge with work done on other issues involving young men, such as disability, homelessness and substance use. Extra resources are not necessary but changes in existing practices are. Baljeet Singh Gill (2001) examines the dichotomy between providing social education to all young men and responding to pressure from politicians, managers and communities to police them. He looks at the issue of the power that men have in the youth service, and suggests they need to change and give some of it up if real change is to happen. This has always been the case – male youth officers will often pay lip service to girls' work for example until the issue of appointments, particularly at a senior level, is raised. Then, it is 'impossible to discriminate' and another man is appointed. Singh Gill (2001) also criticises the way that male workers exercise power and control over young men, particularly when undertaking outdoor activities. He advocates issue based work with young men in residential settings, where workers and young people can make a contract about the work and focus on issues important to being male. This will involve the young men taking personal risks and workers taking professional ones but would hopefully 'transform the quality of the relationships they have with each other'.

Gay and lesbian young people

There was no mention of the needs of young people who were not heterosexual in the Albermarle Report, or during the 1960s. Texts such as Button (1974) stressed the development of sexual relationships between boys and girls in the youth club but no mention was made of same sex relationships. Davies (1999) suggests this group is significant only by its absence from provision which was not considered by policy makers until they were forced to do so by the liberation movements of the 1970s.

In 1974 the DES/NCVYS experimental projects were 'opened up to meet the social needs of homosexual young people'. Youth service publications began to feature articles about gay and lesbian young people. Gay and lesbian youth workers started to organise and in 1977 CYWU agreed to support workers facing discrimination. A number of voluntary organisations of gay young people were formed. The ILEA agreed to allow youth committees to judge funding applications from gay and lesbian groups by the same criteria as all other applicants.

However, the Thompson Committee Report of 1982 made no mention of work with gay and lesbian young people. During the 1980s some local authorities, notably the ILEA, funded some projects but these became problematic with the passing of Section 28 of the Local Government Act outlawing the 'promotion' of homosexuality in 1988. Although, in fact, no cases were ever brought, it succeeded in paralysing the service's response just when the issue had begun to be acknowledged (Davies, 1999). No one seemed quite sure whether it meant provision should not be funded and cautious youth officers stopped many initiatives in their tracks. Youth workers who did not feel comfortable with the issue also had an excuse to ignore it. In 1990 the abolition of the ILEA brought much of the funding to an end anyway.

Davies (1999) suggests that the clause did have the effect of bringing gay and lesbian workers together and a national conference was held in 1988 which led to the formation of a National Association of Lesbian and Gay Youth Workers.

In 1993 Banks found that what little specialist provision existed was concentrated in the larger cities. Most of the work remains in the voluntary sector and funding is often precarious but good work goes on:

> *At the Freedom Youth Project staff had a sound understanding of the needs of gay and lesbian young people, based on a detailed assessment of the young peoples needs and by a system of regular review. They planned programmes with young people and actively involved them in evaluation. Youth workers responded well to individuals and small groups as well as to the full complement of over 25 young people.*
>
> (HMI Report Bristol Youth Service, 2000)

That there is work to be done is clear (Ashby, 2001). Many young people suffer abuse and bullying at school where a homophobic sub-culture can lead to extreme distress and even to suicide attempts. Youth groups can be vital for young people who need a safe space to 'come out' and explore issues with others in the same position. These groups provide an alternative to pubs and clubs and can offer trained youth work support, preferably from gay workers. The venue is important (Ashby, 2001) and needs to be both easy to find and secure.

Work needs also to happen in mixed settings and it is important not to assume that all the members of the youth club are heterosexual – they almost certainly aren't. Ashby asks 'How can we indicate to a young person that we are not homophobic?' She suggests using posters, being careful of language, such as 'partner' rather than boyfriend or girlfriend, and of course challenging homophobic comments. Discussing the issue in an open and confident manner is important as is challenging young people's use of terms such as 'gay' as a term of abuse.

Black young people

As with all issues of equal opportunities the language we use is very important. In using the term 'black young people' to encompass a wide range of ethnicities I am following Webb (2001), when he acknowledges that the terms 'black' and 'white' do not capture the ethnic diversity of the young people we work with and quotes Williams (1993) who feels that generalising from this division is valid as 'the colour of one's skin so profoundly affects the way one is treated.'

The history of youth work with black young people goes back to the 1960s, but although the Albermarle Committee met in the wake of race riots in Nottingham and Notting Hill, they did not look explicitly at the youth service's response to the needs of a multi-cultural society. That had to wait until 1965 when the government set up a committee, chaired by Lord Hunt, to 'consider the part the youth service might play in meeting the needs of young immigrants in England and Wales'. The Hunt Report, *Immigrants and the Youth Service* appeared in 1967. Its major conclusion was that the problem was prejudice and this could only be solved by establishing channels of communication and understanding through personal relationships. Integration was seen as an essential aspiration for society, and therefore for the youth service, and separate provision was frowned on. However, there was debate within the service about how best to cater for the needs of young black people, which often came to the realisation that ethnic groups needed their own space. A report by the Youth Service Information centre, in the early 1970s, stated that 'separate provision is the only way in which some groups and individuals will be able to find sufficient security to step out into a multi-racial society' (quoted in Davies, 1999: 103).

Throughout the 1970s, the youth service was forced to rethink its attitudes by the rise of the black consciousness movement, mounting evidence of discrimination, and racism and riots in major cities. Black youth workers organised themselves and demanded that routes to qualification be opened up, and more indigenous provision be developed and supported. In some places separate clubs or nights were established.

In 1980 the Commission for Racial Equality published figures showing the low take up of youth provision by young black people and called for a radical review of the service.

The Thompson report of 1982 recognised the experience of racism among young black people and recommended that youth work:

- Should become fully multi-cultural in its outlook and curriculum.
- Use its capacity to campaign for equal opportunity and appropriate community development.
- Introduce positive action into its management practices.

It recognised that separate provision for young black people was needed to respond to need. Local Authorities and their youth services developed anti-racist policies.

The Youth and Race in the Inner City Project grew out of a multi-racial project set up by NAYC. Its 1983 report *In the Service of Black Youth* (John, 1981) contended that youth clubs were part of a series of local settings within which young black people were attempting to respond to their social conditions.

John (1981) criticised the youth service as having a 'predominately pathological' view of young black people, and not providing the right sort of input to meet their needs. The focus of the youth service was on 'alienated and disaffected' black youth who needed to be 'returned to the fold' of mainstream society. He felt black youth workers were colluding in this view. The report was an indictment of youth club work where it was felt that the youth workers in the clubs were 'totally redundant', acting more as caretakers than youth workers. His report also raised questions about the age of young people using facilities. Many authorities excluded those over 21, while John felt this was to 'cream off' one or two to become youth workers, rather than encouraging community use and ownership. He felt that 'young blacks have established the principle that youth clubs are what the people who use them want to make of them and *not* what providers and those they employ determine' (John, 1983: 207).

Research had shown greater use of youth clubs by black young people than by white. Willis (1985) suggested that they used clubs as territory within which to express cultural preferences and establish a collective identity. Kealy (1988) felt this offered the youth service a new understanding of participation, allowing young people to manage their own affairs.

In 1986 NYB produced a guide to anti-racist youth work for white workers. They found that workers were using opportunities that came up in conversation in clubs to challenge attitudes, and were also trying to create opportunities, visiting black clubs, having discussions or using exercises, such as banning people with blue eyes from the club. However, an investigation for NYB (Chauhan, 1987) concluded that any change in provision was largely down to individual workers and black pressure rather than a strategic plan. Too often the work did not go beyond offering experiences of different cultures, the steel bands and samosas of Chauhan's title. More trained black workers were however, beginning to enter the system from apprenticeship schemes and other routes. Black voluntary organisations began to get DES funding, such as the National Association of Muslim Youth.

A report on youth work with black and Asian young people by HMI in 1990 was positive about the work going on in many areas, and the way that voluntary bodies and local authorities were trying to make their provision attractive to black and Asian young people and promote equal opportunities policies. However, at times of cuts, the development of separate work often meant cuts in existing budgets or the quest for short term funding such as Section 11. One of the problems with accessing short term funding, for small voluntary groups, is the infrastructure and knowledge needed to support any bid, which may be difficult for ethnic communities to access. This is a particular problem for groups wishing to do youth work in the voluntary sector, and they should be given support from youth officers to access funding.

Davies (1999) feels that the youth service, certainly in comparison with other public services, had come a long way towards examining its inherent racism, even before the Macpherson report into the Lawrence enquiry of

1999, which revealed the police's refusal to contemplate the existence of institutional racism. However, he acknowledges that the youth service remained unsure of how to do 'black youth work'. As Webb (2001) argues, it is essential to locate targeted work with young black people within a critical framework that acknowledges the impact of institutional racism on the way services are provided. Many services designed for black young people problematise them as offenders, drug takers, truants, non-achievers. Webb (2001: 13) demonstrates the cycle that youth service providers can find themselves in, reinforcing the marginalisation of black young people, as black young people are made to feel different, special and problematic. The realities of the lives of young black people, who experience racism every day, need to be reflected in the services provided to them. Webb (2001) talks about the need for holistic practice in work with young black people, respecting the totality of their lives, involving respect for human rights, for different cultures and religions, commitment to anti-discriminatory practices and empowerment and participation. This work should be the bedrock of youth club practice everywhere.

Youth clubs have often provided a safe space for young black people, particularly for groups such as young Asian women who would not be able to attend mixed provision, or by offering opportunities for groups from different backgrounds to meet on neutral territory. Specialist work, such as black history groups, provide for the needs of particular groups at different times. Youth club workers should be concerned if the club is only used by one racial group, and find out what other provision exists in the area for other groups. A racially mixed staff team, posters and a programme of activities that demonstrate a commitment to diversity, and posters and publicity in different languages and so on are all important. Advertising for staff in newspapers with a mainly black readership demonstrates a commitment to the issue. The club should demonstrate its equal opportunities commitment before you walk through the door!

Following the riots in Bradford, the Home Office has been keen to promote cross cultural contact and to set up initiatives which get people from different communities working together. (YPN, May 2003: 14–20; Thomas, 2003). Youth clubs have been involved in trying to bring the white and ethnic communities together. In some communities in the North of England, young people have few chances to meet people from different cultural backgrounds except in youth clubs. This can help with community cohesion (see Chapter 8). It is also important that youth clubs explore these issues with white young people, and exchanges from rural areas to cities can be really helpful, allowing young people to try new experiences and meet other young people with different life experiences – but lots in common.

Disabled young people

Although the Albermarle building plans made no provision for the needs of people with disabilities, who might want to use the premises, youth clubs were reasonably accessible, usually being single storey buildings with large doors. Some specialist and innovative work with disabled young people developed in the 1960s (Davies, 1999) and several voluntary sector organisations were formed for young people with learning difficulties, such as the Elfrida Rathbone Society, and in 1966 the Federation of Gateway Clubs. The main attempt at integration of young people with disabilities into the mainstream facilities was pioneered by the NAYC in 1957 and by the mid 1970s there was a nationwide network of clubs known as PHAB, Physically Handicapped and Able Bodied (www.phabengland.org.uk) which is still very active.

Despite the 1970 Chronically Sick and Disabled Persons Act requiring local authorities 'to make recreational and educational facilities available outside the home' (Davies, 1999), the needs of young people with disabilities were not really considered in the youth service through the 1970s. The youth work press engaged in the debate about language and the shift from a 'medical' model to a 'social' model of disability. In 1974 the National Youth Assembly conference concluded that not much integration was happening.

In 1981, The United Nations International Year of the Disabled, the National Youth Bureau identified integration as 'the key to improved opportunities in education, employment, leisure and social activities for the disabled'.

A 1989 NACYS working party found that there was minimal provision other than that offered by Gateway or PHAB (DES, 1989). The resulting recommendations included suggestions for the development of complementary specialist and integrated facilities. Another report by HMI confirmed these findings and found provision constrained by lack of resources, with good work being largely down to individuals on the ground. By 1992 more local authorities had issued policy statements and later in the 1990s a disabled workers' network was set up.

Integration

It remains the case that the appearance of young people with disabilities, of whatever kind, is still an unusual event in most clubs. As Kutner and Factor explain (2001) there is a difference between integration and inclusion in that:

> *. . . integration focuses on whether the young person is ready to become involved in mainstream youth provision and inclusion starts from the perspective that youth provision is accepting of all young people and should ensure that everyone has a sense of ownership and belonging.*
>
> (p3)

The Disability Act (1995) and the Disability Rights Commission set up in 2000 to enforce it, should encourage workers to improve their premises, as it is now unlawful to discriminate against disabled people. This, plus the Human Rights Amendment of October 2000 should make a reality of the right of every young person to take part in youth provision. The issue of resources will always be raised, but there are often funds available for building adaptations, particularly for employed workers, and social services may well have funds for transport and staff under the Children's Act 1989. This is a good way of building interagency links. The Special Educational Needs and Disability Act 2001 (SENDA) makes it illegal to discriminate against disabled young people in education. If a young person comes to a youth club it is an offence to turn them away or to offer less of a service because of their disability. Money has been made available to allow the statutory service to respond to their new duties under the Act. This was £7m in 2002–03 rising to £8m in each of the years from 2003–04 to 2005–06.The Minister for Youth services, Ivan Lewis, announcing this to the Association of Principal Youth Officers, said:

> *I hope that all of you will maximise the opportunity provided by this funding to increase the menu of opportunity available to disabled young people in your areas.*

Certainly some have done (*Young People Now*, 30 June–6 July: 6). Liverpool City Council have been doing an audit of youth service buildings and are hoping to recruit young people with disabilities to become accredited auditors.

The needs of young people with disabilities

Use of the youth club by young people with disabilities is not going to happen just by making premises accessible and sitting back and waiting for young people to arrive. As Kutner and Factor (2001) state, ensuring equal access to provision is about being flexible enough to meet changing needs. Recent research by the Joseph Rowntree Foundation (www.jrf.org.uk) found that a major source of frustration for young disabled people lay in the gap they perceived between the rhetoric of the Disability Discrimination Act, and their common experience of being denied access to public transport, buildings and open spaces. Also, whether young disabled people were in special or mainstream school, they ended up feeling isolated from their peers. These young people wanted to be involved in mainstream provision but also valued the relationships they made at specialist provision. This is certainly borne out by my experience of working in both. Support is needed to enable disabled young people to enjoy leisure activities in terms of transport, physical help and resources. However, it should not have to come from their parents at a time when most able-bodied young people are asserting their independence.

The Rowntree Report concludes:

> *. . . in all conversations with young disabled people on the subject of inclusive leisure, the emphasis has been on friendship and fun. Whilst opportunities to try out a range of leisure activities and pursuits are appreciated, it is the opportunity to be in mutually valued relationships that young disabled people identify as the key to the possibility of their inclusion in mainstream culture. Leisure provides a natural building ground for the development of relationships based on a common interest; placing such valued relationships in the mainstream allows discriminatory and oppressive attitudes to be broken down as natural enjoyment and positive relationships become visible.*

The needs of young people with disabilities are not fundamentally different from those of able bodied young people. All young people want to talk about sex, want to go on roller coasters, to the pictures or for a Chinese meal whether they are in a wheelchair or not and, although things have improved recently, it's important to check for access. If young people with disabilities start to join in the life of the club at weekends and on holidays then it is important to check what is needed by way of specialist help or to make sure staff are trained if necessary and comfortable about helping young people go to the toilet etc. But it's possible to undertake most activites – including camping if you're prepared to be adaptable. Much of the concern, about making our provision fully accessible and encouraging young people with disabilities to use it, is a fear of the unknown. Disabled people have been segregated too much from the rest of society, for example research by Whizz-Kiddz in 2001 found that two thirds of able bodied young people have never even spoken to a physically disabled person of their own age (*Young People Now*, 22.1.03).

Specialist provision

Just as there is a need for specialist provision for other groups, young people with disabilities often want to meet on their own. 'It's just more relaxing, I don't feel stared at as a freak all the time.' However, it is important to recognise the differing needs of such groups. Young deaf people may want space to communicate with each other and deaf staff in their own language or young people with learning difficulties may need advocacy from workers in getting their needs met. Many of these groups are looking for a chance to explore common issues and often can develop into political bodies.

Recruitment

Initially, finding disabled young people to include in the youth club may be difficult. Young people with disabilities are often hidden in society, and from their peers, and assume that provision for young people does not apply to them. When I first tried to attract young people from our local special school to our holiday scheme, I was told by one parent that although our scheme had been running in previous years she did not think it was for her daughter who had a disability. It was not until I visited the school, and sent targeted letters home, that disabled young people started to attend the scheme. Work to integrate disabled young people into a youth club is by its nature interagency work, as youth workers will need help in making contact with local disabled young people. This often involves making contact with parents who may be understandably wary about letting their son or daughter attend a youth club. Social services can prove invaluable in helping to organise transport.

Activities

Once young people are at the club it is important to find activities in which they can participate on equal terms. It is important not to limit the programme solely to games and activities specifically designed for disabled young people: most things are possible. Once young people with disabilities are part of the life of the club, able bodied young people will be keen to help them get involved in everything that goes on, including helping on trips away from the club.

It's usually possible to borrow minibuses, barges and sailing boats specially adapted for wheelchair use. Many residential centres have facilities, but it's important to check the quality first – it's no good having a specially adapted toilet and shower if there is no heating in the room.

Staffing

As Kutner and Factor (2001) report, youth workers do not require any special skills to promote an inclusive environment but they do need support, resources and training; and, above all, experience and the chance to reflect upon it.

It is important to advertise widely, especially in the disability press, when recruiting the staff team: disabled youth workers will provide powerful models for all young people, and enable those with disabilities to feel more at home.

Having a designated worker whose role is to help introduce young people with disabilities to the club may be a good idea, at least to start off with, but they must not be the person who does all the work. They should be a catalyst around whom other workers can develop their practice. Training in skills such as Braille and sign language, including Makaton (used with young people with learning difficulties), and in safety measures such as training in lifting will help workers feel more confident.

Hopefully there should be no young people that you absolutely could not work with, but extra workers, volunteers or facilities may be required if you are working with very severely disabled young people.

Access

Ideally every club should be accessible to all young people in the area, but this is rarely a reality in the old buildings used by youth clubs. For instance, in Bristol, in 2000, seven out of eighteen buildings maintained by the youth service were inaccessible, or had limited access for people with mobility difficulties (Bristol Youth Service Ofsted Inspection, March 2000). At least one of these, Brentry Youth Centre, has since been made accessible and given a refit using Transforming Youth Work money (*Young People Now*, 27.6.04). However, it is important not to postpone doing anything until you have perfect access. Some older buildings will remain in use if alterations to make them wheelchair friendly are thought unreasonable (YPN, 22.1.03). Much can be done quite simply with ramps or by the use of Braille and large print signs and notices, for example. If you have the luxury of starting off in a new building it is important to get a proper audit of accessibility undertaken: those brightly coloured coffee bar seats may look cool but fixed seating makes it impossible for people in wheelchairs to get to the table, sunken areas likewise. It's important that young people with disabilities aren't treated as second class by being made to enter the building round the back or needing to ask for assistance to open heavy doors. Toilets should be accessible for both sexes and a separate toilet 'for the disabled' doesn't help people feel included.

Working holistically

Youth workers aspire to see young people first and foremost as young people and avoid labels. However, they need to be aware of the discrimination that young people can face, from being young but also from being black, or disabled, or female or gay, or sometimes a combination of these. Different cultures have different attitudes to issues such as homosexuality and disability, which can make life even more difficult for young people. The youth service is uniquely placed to offer positive role models and above all space for young people to explore their own identity in association with their peers. Youth clubs cannot claim to be delivering association if they are excluding members of the peer group, whether the exclusion is deliberate or not.

What is depressing is that one can still read news stories such as that recently in *Young People Now* (7–13th July 2004) about Hertfordshire Youth

Service setting up a pilot scheme to integrate disabled young people within mainstream projects, or hear youth work students complaining about the difficulties of getting girls work going. It seems that the work done in the 1980s has still not become embedded as part of practice and the battle for equal opportunities in clubs has to be won all over again for each generation of young people.

Chapter 6

The Management of Youth Club Work

This chapter examines the current issues posed by the notion of management in centre based work, and the role of the youth officer. It also looks at the role of management committees, the importance of training and accountability, how to organise the club and the thorny issue of evaluation. While not directly managing the work, the National Associations of Youth Clubs, the National Youth Agency and the Community and Youth Workers Union have important roles to play which are also examined in this chapter.

Post Albermarle (Ministry of Education, 1960) the loose network of voluntary organisations that had made up the youth service was superseded by bureaucratic structures, created to manage a provision which was being paid for out of taxation. This led to an emphasis on professionalism and tighter controls over face-to-face work, so that full-time workers often describe themselves as managers today. A full-time worker running a busy youth club can inevitably be seen as its manager, but the management skills needed in terms of making relationships and networking, working autonomously, have no great mystique, and workers basically need to be good face-to-face workers with staff and above all with young people.

During the 1960s Davies (1999) considers that 'we and them' notions of management were largely unknown in the service. In the 1970s more posts were introduced that were managerial in content, meaning that space for workers to exercise their own professional judgement was reduced. Before the 1980s, as Jeffs and Smith (1988) point out, there was little discussion of the practice of management in the youth work literature or indeed in the major youth service reports. However, after Thompson (1982) it became a major theme. The Thompson Report diagnosed the main problem of the youth service as poor management, arising out of a lack of training of workers for management tasks. The lack of management training on initial training courses continues to be a concern of youth officers, and one recent initiative was the development of specific training for youth service managers. In recent years managers have often been sent on Diploma and Certificate in Management courses, which often have only limited relevance to the needs of the job of a youth work manager.

Youth Service Officers constantly complain that youth workers need management skills but are rarely specific about what they actually mean. The definition of management can be debated and is often confused with administration, i.e. filling in forms etc. These tasks have undoubtedly multiplied over the last decade but whether the service or individual units are 'better' managed is difficult to assess, as is whether this style of management has improved the youth work itself. Jeffs and Smith suggested in 1988 that part of the reason for management becoming such a rallying call was the cutbacks in public expenditure – the consequent need to attract outside funding involved increased form filling and bureaucracy. Currently the stable core funding available for youth work is significantly smaller than the total funding recorded (Merton et al., 2005). There was also the transplantation of managerial methods from industry, proposed as the solution to improving public services. As several writers have pointed out (Bloxham, 1993; Bamber, 2000; Smith, 2001) there is a fundamental problem with applying business models to welfare services. This 'new managerialism' has restricted workers ability to be autonomous and respond to need, leaving practice largely unchanged. It does, however, enhance the control of the central manager. The process of centralisation has also led to an increase in time spent in meetings and decreasing time spent in face-to-face work. What seems to have been lost in all this concentration on management is any idea of how to improve practice through supervision and support.

There is also an issue with services now appointing managers who are not JNC qualified and indeed may have no experience of youth club work. The lack of managers who are not white, male and middle class in many parts of the country is also important in the context of support for workers (see Chapter 5).

Youth officers, supervision and support

The role of a full-time worker has always been isolated. Supervision and support is vital for all workers, especially those operating outside the statutory sector who may receive no formal management. A recent NYA survey of OFSTED reports indicates that less than a quarter of services have satisfactory supervision practices (Jenkinson, 2002). Jenkinson explains the three-fold nature of supervision:

- To support the worker.
- To identify and pursue staff development needs.
- To provide a context in which the work is monitored.

Unfortunately the monitoring purpose often takes over. Many managers tend to look on supervision as something only needed by poorly performing staff. If used by management in this way it inevitably becomes regarded with suspicion by workers. However, Jeffs and Smith (1988) suggest that many youth workers resist being told what to do. In their view, in the 1980s youth work was often seen as offering the 'opportunity to maximise freedom and minimise accountability'.

There has been a problem with the definition of youth officers' roles, for example, some are even called advisors and are therefore seen by workers and management committees as having only an advisory role. A confusion exists between the levels at which they operate as demonstrated by Bradford and Day (1991). Are youth officers engaged at a policy development level or in day-to-day management? *The Impact of Youth Work Study* (Merton et al., 2005) found managers struggling with the balance between strategic and operational management. Local authorities vary tremendously in the number of full-time workers line managed by each officer. The commitment of officers to adequately perform supervision, attend management committees and monitor club work by visiting can require them to work extremely long hours.

It is no wonder then that supervision gets neglected, or delegated to a nearby senior worker, especially when the travel involved in some geographically dispersed authorities can be very time consuming. The problem with supervision by a senior worker is that they may not have sufficient overview of the context necessary for Jenkinson's third point to be effective. It also takes senior workers away from their own centres: many so-called full-time centres are actually run by part-time staff while the full-time worker has an area role in working with other agencies and supervising other staff. It can also be argued that youth workers need not only managerial but also non-managerial supervision. Some authorities included this in staff development budgets in the 1980s, but now it seems largely to have disappeared. Youth workers need this time for reflection and must ensure that it happens, through a voluntary arrangement with colleagues if necessary. A more encouraging trend over the last few years has been the increase in supervision offered to part-time staff: now paid for in many authorities as part of their JNC pay scale. But cutting hours of opening to ensure staff supervision needs very careful thinking about if the needs of young people are to remain the top priority. The volume and quality of supervision actually happening is difficult to assess. Full-time workers who are not receiving good supervision will lack a good model from which to work and are unlikely to become good supervisors themselves. This is often the situation that youth work students find on placement.

The introduction of formal briefing and debriefing in clubs has been very useful, where organised and managed properly, and not taken as an excuse to turn up late or sit around chatting.

Management committees

In the years before youth work became a recognised profession, superintendents were used to run the club on a day-to-day basis. Bunt and Gargrave (1980) feel that the apparent abdication of leadership by the Victorian middle classes to paid superintendents, mostly from a lower social class, is something of a paradox. They suggest that this was really an adaptation of the nanny principle! The superintendents carried out the mundane chores and exercised discipline and control over the members, but the real decision makers were the matriarchal and patriarchal figures who paid their wages. In time it proved possible to exercise authority and shape policies through the evolution of Club Management Committees which 'institutionalised the power wielding of the establishment type personalities' (Bunt and Gargrave, 1980: 24). Even today, these committees often have a great deal of power, to hire and fire staff, to agree expenditure and to make policies.

The power and influence of a management committee varies from area to area and club to club. In voluntary sector clubs they may well be the employing body, even if funds come from the local authority. Many of these committees have a long history and some members have been involved with the club in various capacities all their lives.

How active the committee is depends on the policies of the local authority, the constitution of the club, the attitude of the members and how active they want to be and how the youth worker uses them. Committees usually consist of a local councillor or two, local worthies such as the vicar, a head teacher or a bank manager – very useful for the position of treasurer – perhaps some former members, the local police officer, the LEA youth officer and a couple of young people. In smaller clubs it may be a few interested parents, but the club will need to devise a constitution if it wants to set up a bank account and affiliate to the youth service or a voluntary organisation. Voluntary sector youth clubs may well have a board of trustees instead of a management committee and there are certainly some creative models where young people are heavily involved and have been instrumental in setting up the club. The most successful clubs usually have a powerful management committee, which can not only argue effectively for resources from the local authority but also raise funds themselves. Finding a good chair for the committee is vital. If young people and members of the community are going to want to come to meetings, they must be run efficiently. It is important that the chair is not picked just because they are a local worthy – they may just be adding the club to their list of good works. Many chairs also like to see the club as their own empire, and will appear only at meetings to dispense wisdom. Meetings may become a farce where the worker has spent hours writing a report only to have it dismissed in two minutes before the meeting is speedily wound up in time for Coronation Street. Conversely, the worker may be quizzed interminably on every detail until past midnight. Somewhere between these models there is the efficient committee where members have a real investment in the club. Particularly in small one night a week clubs, the time spent by the youth worker in recruitment and retention of a good committee will reap dividends in the future. Members need to feel wanted, and should be asked to visit and help out in the club where possible, but it should be made clear to them that their role does not extend to bawling at young people or staff! Members can be drawn from ex-youth club members and other groups using the centre but the main criterion should be an interest in young people. They should also have a commitment to keeping the club used by young people as much as possible, in spite of the temptation to go for the money which can be earned from renting the premises to adult groups.

Accountability

Youth club workers play a complex, demanding and pivotal role in managing the interface between the club, the local authority and other agencies. It is important that workers are able to avoid being used by the management committee or the local authority as a stick with which to beat one another. This can be especially difficult where workers attached to voluntary organisations have their salary paid by the local authority, are line managed by the youth officer, but are seen by the management committee as *their* worker. Workers may well decide not to spend time developing their committees to avoid these type of conflicts, and perhaps also preferring to keep hold of the power. This is a symptom of what Jeffs and Smith (1988) described as a failure of workers to attend to questions of local and community accountability. They also suggest that many workers fail to appreciate the nature of work with adults – they have chosen the work to work with young people and resist the idea that they need to have credibility with adults as well. There may be a gender issue here as well, since full-time workers were traditionally male. Spence (1988) suggests that youth club work panders to the masculine ego of full-time male workers. The worker becomes the leader of the gang, in effect, and resents other adults being involved.

One of the problems with management committees, as Bunt and Gargrave pointed out in 1980 is that information about wider developments in the service and nationally is not available to them – a crucial issue that may lead to a lack of new initiatives in some clubs. However, as Bunt and Gargrave suggest, it is a paradox that trained professional workers function best if subject to the checks and balances of untrained management committee members. A parallel could be drawn here with school governors. Management committees are often seen by youth workers as a cross to be borne rather than a support. Workers who want to keep their freedom do not work to enable the management committees to function effectively. Some committees consist of people who like to be in positions of power and influence, without needing to do very much. There are many instances of enthusiastic new youth workers ground down by a management committee's inability to welcome new ideas. Battles such as trying to get the management committee of a boys club to admit girls have not endeared me to the beasts.

It is interesting that a 1973 survey by Lowe for the London Union of Youth Clubs (cited by Bunt and Gargrave, 1980) concluded that a new look at selection procedures for management committee members was essential. Certainly her idea that all appointees should have a genuine concern for club work, have roots in the local community and bring valuable expertise to the committee is a good one, it is a pity that nothing really seems to have changed since then. In many cases this has been due to LEA managers not really wanting to have effective management committees, which might challenge their authority. Managers often prefer projects such as detached work where they have a more hands-on management role and do not have to work with local committees. The idea of 'strong management' could help to explain the lack of youth officers' enthusiasm in some clubs, where they walk a tightrope between the needs of the service and the commitment of managers to their local club. Officers have found it impossible to close clubs, which they feel have out stayed their usefulness, in the teeth of local political opposition, particularly where the club premises are used extensively by adult groups. Those badminton clubs and bridge clubs not to mention the canary societies can pack quite a political punch!

Training

Clubs have always depended on adult workers, voluntary or paid, face-to-face or behind the scenes. Bunt and Gargrave (1980) felt that it was self-evident that they must have specific qualities and social attitudes.

The debate about the social origins of workers has been long running. The drive to professionalism, started under Albermarle, was criticised as undermining the long volunteering tradition of the service and excluding working class women and black people by concentrating resources on full-time workers, mainly white men (Davies, 1999). Davies went on to point out the detrimental effect that this failure to attract substantial numbers of women would have on the service in the long term. As mixed gender provision became popular, the existing male domination of the workforce led to girls being seen as a problem, and work with them being marginalised. As these workers were promoted into management positions during the 1970s, the dominance of male attitudes and management styles continued. In 1970 it was estimated that only 3 per cent of full-time workers were female, so that even with 25 per cent of entrants to courses in 1977 being female, this imbalance was set to continue. However, this pendulum seems to have swung the other way now with the majority of youth work students being female.

Much of the debate about making training more accessible in the 1970s and 1980s was to ensure that full-time youth workers came from the same type of background and had similar experiences to those of the young people they worked with. The apprenticeship schemes, set up in the early 1980s, along with a widening participation agenda, encouraged more women and people from ethnic minorities to train, but they were often faced with discrimination in the work place and a diminishing availability of support and supervision. The introduction of these schemes, 17 in all, plus new availability of part-time and full-time routes to qualification, meant that there were many more qualified workers by the early 1990s, posing the potential problem of a glut of qualified staff (Davies, 1999). Today, however, there are difficulties in filling posts, particularly in centre based work, and a survey in 2000 by CYWU showed that many vacancies had to be re-advertised several times. Often unqualified workers are appointed and sent on part-time training courses, or the new Foundation degrees. This is similar to the position in the 1960s when the lack of qualified staff led many services to appoint unqualified part-time workers and send them on the new training courses opening up around the country.

Part-time Workers

Training for part-time workers and volunteers has always been an issue in the service. Where clubs have been desperate for staff, part-time workers have often been taken on after a brief interview establishing that they want to work with young people and, more recently, a criminal records check. Training has been seen as something that workers got on the job or did in their own time, and it was only recently that many authorities paid for it. The Bessy Report of 1962, following Albermarle, tried to find a common element to all youth work, whether done by voluntary organisations or the state. The Butters and Newell Report of 1978 was one of the few systematic attempts to analyse the nature of youth work (Davies, 1999), which it found to be fragmented and variable in quality but made no recommendations for action. Thompson (1982) recognised the valuable work done by part-timers but did not really look at their training. A 1983 survey found that qualifications awarded as a result of part-time training run by some local authorities were not being recognised by others. The *Starting from Strengths Report* of 1984 advocated that training should be grounded in workers actual experience, so that they could build on existing strengths. This led to reviews by local authorities of their training and led to the rise of portfolio based courses. These were not always as rigorous as could be wished, as an OFSTED report on training suggested in 2002. A network of Regional Accrediting and Moderating Panels (RAMPs) set up during the 1990s led to the part-time worker qualifications being recognised as valid by a group of local authorities. The establishment of Paulo, the national training organisation, led to the establishment of National Occupational Standards for Youth Work and, following the demise of the RAMPs in 2003, NVQ/VRQ qualifications at levels 2 and 3 in youth work being developed for part-time training. There will also be a Modern Apprenticeship in youth work for the 16 plus age range (http://www.nya.org.uk).

All of these initiatives treat youth work very much as though it was one body of knowledge and skills, and yet its practice varies considerably – the needs of a club worker for training are different from those of a detached worker, for instance in organisation and programming in the club. The same applies to the training of full-time staff. It is possible for workers to become qualified without ever having set foot in a youth club and I feel this is wrong, if youth club work is still the core of youth work practice. Unfortunately it is no longer seen as such. Current training courses have to comply with the National Occupational Standards but they are supposed to cover a huge range of practice.

Organisation and administration

This is about the day-to-day running of the club. The important thing is that the club is there when the young people want it, but also that they know what to expect:

> *You have to keep your word with kids, do what you say you'll do and the time you'll do it so they know they can rely on you. If you're going to be a youth worker you've got to mix with the kids, join in.*
>
> (Truman and Brent, 1995)

This last is important; you can't run a youth club by sitting in the office. For a full-time worker, the daytime should be for meetings and phone calls – clerical help is invaluable in this context. Youth workers should spend their time doing youth work (which is after all why they went into it) but this does not mean that all administration can be neglected. Ingram and Harris (2001) provide some excellent advice and suggestions for coping with administration and organising your time, largely for the full-time worker. However, it is even more important if you are running a one night a week club that you get other people involved in the administration.

Finance and fundraising

Youth workers are not always particularly interested in the money side of their work, but it is the area where they can easily run into problems. One of the worst sights for managers is a worker's desk drawer filled with receipts and scribbled notes. Keeping the books can easily be delegated, and there are often local people who would like to help the youth club but not actually have to come to it! Youth workers, especially in the voluntary sector, have always been involved in fundraising at Christmas bazaars and jumble sales, running sponsored events, to raise some extra cash for a trip away or a piece of equipment. For example, when raising money for a trip to France, the girls from my club raised money by using a contraption to 'Drench the Wench' at various local club summer fairs. We also tried 'Flood the Stud' with less success! However, this type of funding is very small beer compared to the large sums that can be got from the National Lottery Foundation, Children in Need, or the government SRB, Children's Fund and holiday Splash money. Increasingly it is seen as part of a full-time workers job to chase funding, often involving a great deal of work preparing bids. Edwards and Hatch (2003) found that youth work providers often have to draw on many different sources of funding in order to provide activities for young people, each time meeting different criteria and filling in different applications. This may raise ethical dilemmas for the worker (Jeffs and Smith, 1999) and the reliance on short-term funding, often tied to the delivery of a particular programme, brings special problems due to the amount of time it takes and the instability it brings (*Young People Now*, 19.3.03: 16) also the amount of monitoring required. It can be argued that project work feeds the decline of open access club work as it is so much easier to demonstrate its outcomes.

Jeffs and Smith ask (1999) whether some sources of money are ethically unacceptable. It is important that club workers think hard about these issues. The merits of having a new building on a Private Finance Initiative, for example, may be tempting but they come with strings attached. In PFI built schools, community use is restricted and very expensive. The raising of funds usually involves painting exaggerated images of young people; I well remember some young people I took on a trip to the Lake District obtaining funding from the Prince's Trust by writing heart rending letters on the Monty Python lines of 'I live in a shoebox!' and any fundraising involving young people with disabilities will end up with the press painting young people as tragic victims or brave heroes. Jeffs and Smith (1999) feel that this stigmatises young people and panders to popular prejudices. Another problem is that the voluntary relationship young people have with a youth worker implies a moral authority on the part of the worker, who will need to pay attention to their integrity, consistency and principles. For instance, youth clubs need to think about what messages they are giving young people if they take funding from the sellers of fast food, or sell junk food and also run healthy eating campaigns.

The nightly programme

The design of the Albermarle buildings was supposed to help the leader be in touch with all that was going on a on a particular night, providing an uninterrupted space or a series of linked spaces (Ministry of Education, 1961). Certainly it does help the workers if the area is not too large, but ideally there should be some space where young people can work on a project, or discuss an issue, on their own or with a member of staff away from the general mêlée, and it should not be the office. Button's (1975) methodology of small group work in centres meant that the workers reported to the full-time worker on the progress of the work with their group, and received support from them. The full-time worker's role therefore was to co-ordinate the work and to keep in touch with what was going on during the evening. Planning the programme should be done in conjunction with the young people or delegated to a members' committee, but in the end it is the centre based worker's responsibility to make sure there is plenty going on.

One of the important roles of the full-time worker or leader in charge is to make sure that staff know what they are doing during the evening, and do not just end up chatting to each other at the coffee bar. Giving guidelines to staff on jobs for the evening at the beginning of the session is vital and Button's (1975) method means that some staff are working with a group for at least part of the evening. Others will have a roving role, overseeing activities and picking up issues as they occur. There is nothing worse than having to break up an important conversation with a young person to find a new table tennis ball. Everyday concerns should be dealt with by the young people or a designated member of staff.

Marketing and publicity

While young people choose to come to the club, they need information on which to base this choice. Youth workers should think about the basics of marketing and publicity – getting your message across and letting people know what is going on is vital. A 1995 survey of participation in the youth service by the DES found that 25 per cent of young people were not sure what the youth service had to offer. Even in these days of the internet, not all clubs have got themselves on-line, and in the lists of local authority facilities available it is often impossible to find out such simple facts as the club opening hours. Understandably, youth workers don't want solely to be judged by the numbers coming through the door, but it is important to make some attempt to publicise the club's activities. The local press are always glad to fill their pages with ready made copy and writing this can be a useful exercise for the young people themselves. Young people usually love having their picture in the paper, too.

Thinking about who the customer is and how to attract them can involve:

- Looking at the club from an outsider's position.
- Checking out the competition.
- Offering free entrance if young people bring a friend.
- Getting rid of the entrance charge completely.
- Opening at different times.

If you do something new, make sure people know about it, 'hot food now available', 'now wheelchair accessible' etc.

Visiting local schools and colleges can be valuable, as can stalls in the local shopping centre.

Make sure the youth club is visible from the road: many is the time that I have walked or driven past the club that I was actually looking for! The youth service could learn from MacDonald's here – never be difficult to spot.

If you wander in off the street, one of the first things you would like to see about a youth club is that there are lots of activities planned. Activities within the club need publicising, and a weekly and monthly events list should be prominently displayed.

Recording

Getting staff to record their work is vital. Some clubs use a general book, others have a system of forms, or a recorded debrief. It is important is that it is kept simple and that it actually happens. Staff and volunteers do not want to spend a long time filling in forms at the end of the night. A daily message book is also vital for last minute thoughts. Local authorities often want to be able to monitor the work, using statistics and recordings of the work, as part of the evaluation but all workers should reflect on their practice and be given time to do so.

Evaluation

One of the early attempts to evaluate youth club work was by Lesley Sewell, who was general secretary of the National Association of Mixed and Girls Clubs from 1953 to 1966. She asked how one might judge the quality and value of youth clubs objectively , by looking at the objectives of club work, which she defined as: 'to help girls and boys though their leisure time activities so to develop their physical, mental and spiritual capacities that they may grow to full maturity as individuals and members of society' (Sewell, 1966).

She felt it had to be done by visiting clubs, and observing how workers and young people related to each other, and how much community spirit there was. Much of this she acknowledges to be intangible but aspects such as the programme are visible to appropriate inspection. She acknowledges the well known phenomenon in club work where the club is really busy and the best work happens the night before an inspection! She asks 'Is assessment possible?' Sewell felt that one of the best ways was to listen to the club leader, not only what they said but their attitude. She concludes by asking how one can assess the value of a chance word or a seemingly trivial act of friendship. And yet 'something has happened – which will be woven into the fabric of the spirit and one day bear fruit in a new field of relationships' (Sewell, 1966).

In *Kids at the Door Revisited* Holman (2000) revisits the young people he worked with from 1976 to 1986, to demonstrate that it is possible to see long-term benefits of involvement in youth work, as many workers have always argued. For example:

> *We were safe and we had something to do every night. It made me a more responsible person. We could talk about anything. The club not only helped us it helped our parents and teachers too.*
>
> *I remember if you had a problem you could talk to the leaders. Kids today are looking for the same good facilities and leadership that we had.*
>
> (Sharpe, 2004)
>
> *The club made me more tolerant, taught mixing, I learnt to socialise, made me want to be a leader, more responsible.*
>
> (Tewkesbury ex-members quoted in Ballard and Wright, 1994)
>
> *It was the highlight of our lives, locally.*
>
> (Truman and Brent, 1995)
>
> *I feel that the youth club has played a much more important role in my development that school ever did. School gave me academic qualifications. My own experiences, both inside and outside the youth club, stand me in better stead. The youth club opened doors for me.*
>
> (Standing Conference of Youth Organisations in Northern Ireland, 1987)

These quotes demonstrate positive evaluations of a youth club. As Bunt and Gargrave pointed out, in 1980, evaluation is difficult because much of the benefit of the work may not be seen or recognised immediately. A useful exercise with any group is to ask them to think of influential adults in their lives or learning experiences. Many youth workers today got into the work because of the inspirational example of their former youth worker. One of my most vivid learning experiences was my first rock climb, I was nearly physically sick at the top but I carried on and ended up qualifying to top rope so that I could give other people the same experience!

The Thatcherite focus on public sector managerialism, outcomes, targets etc. was first felt by the youth service in the early 1990s with the arrival of the Ministerial conferences. There we learnt the meaning of the term 'performance indicators', and were never allowed to forget it. Ingram and Harris (2002) suggest that to evaluate something you need to know what you are trying to do. The lack of clarity about the objectives of youth work has not helped its evaluation.

In 1994 the Ofsted framework for inspecting youth services was produced. This framework, still largely in place though revised in 1997, is concerned to show young people's learning. It does give a clear framework for evaluation, so that the same things are consistently evaluated everywhere, and talks in terms of achievement. However, some of its criteria, such as young people showing evidence of 'confidence, self-esteem and a sense of empowerment; an ability to make choices, influence programmes and events; developing problem solving skills and self-advocacy' are difficult to assess (Inspecting Youth Work, Ofsted: 7).

If, for example, youth work is supposed to increase self-esteem, then we need a clear idea of what self-esteem actually is, and some way to measure it. This particular issue has roused controversy lately when research found that the concept of self-esteem is murky and imprecise. Raising self-esteem is not the key to transforming young people's lives and solving all problems from suicide and self-harm to educational under-achievement and racial prejudice, as had been claimed (Jeffs, 2003). White (2002) suggested that the constant use of 'self-esteem' makes youth work look and sound weak and intuitive, vague and impressionistic, when good youth work clearly is, or should be, robust and testable.

Ofsted

In view of the long term nature of the relationships involved in club work it is often easier to demonstrate an example of planned work with clear learning outcomes (as demanded by Ofsted) in a small group work session than in an open one. If this method of evaluation is to be used then it's not surprising that youth clubs have often been criticised by Ofsted. For instance, Ofsted mean by high standards that there is a clear focus and a planned approach to the work and that young people are able to articulate what they gain as a result of their involvement (www.ofsted.gov.uk). This is a short term approach which can negate the long term relationship-building approach characteristic of youth clubs.

France and Wiles, in their 1997 evaluation of the Youth Action Schemes, were concerned about the lack of systematic collection and analysis of evidence by workers. However, these schemes were one of the first initiatives to ask youth workers, for example, to measure their performance against national priorities such as crime reduction. If we are going to claim achievements for youth work, we need to be able to demonstrate that it was youth work that attained them.

Also, youth clubs are under constant pressure to show that they are worthwhile, but one of the main problems is that they are under funded, so that saying 'it doesn't work' from any particular evaluation perspective, may be an invalid conclusion.

Methods

Youth club work has been notoriously difficult to evaluate. There are quantitative methods of course, such as numbers attending broken down by age, gender and race. Recordings of practice are essential to be able to describe what actually happened in the work. Certainly a nightly diary filled in by all staff should be part of normal practice, and should not be a chore if combined with a debrief of the night, and a discussion as to how to progress.

Many services nowadays have developed models of evaluation based on an idea of steps, with young people entering the process at one end and leaving at the other (e.g. Huskins, 1996).

Huskins (1996) describes young people progressing from initial involvement through active participation to exiting. We are asked to answer questions about individuals such as; Has this young person 'developed,' and if so by how much? Which stair are they on, and were they there last night? Are they participating? Bradford (2000) in his critique of Huskins' methodology claims that his work aims to 'construct youth work as data'. This is about trying to measure what is, in reality, an informal process, in a formal way. It also defines outcomes rather than negotiating the agenda with young people, thus departing from one of the central tenets of youth work.

The problem with most schemes, though, is that they tend to look at the individual and not the group. Also, not many young people work their way through a scheme as expected. You may feel you are really making headway with a young person, they are really involved in the club, have been decorating it and helping in the juniors, you've stood up for them in court, and then they run away to join the circus or get caught thieving. It's not your fault – it's a problem inherent in the nature of youth work. If youth work starts claiming credit for too much, it must also accept responsibility for those who carry on into a life of crime regardless.

Richardson (1997) describes how, in order to attract funds for deprived areas like the one where he works, workers must take on an agenda from 'outside'. The measured outcomes imposed by new managerialism from the outside, means that the inside views are superseded by the criteria of outside scrutiny. It is difficult to ascertain the content of work that goes on to develop relationships, and trying to measure them changes the relationship.

The latest government advice produced by the Connexions national unit (2002) is that youth service objectives must be SMART i.e. Specific, Measurable, Achievable, Realistic and Time bound. I would contend that much of what we are aiming to do in centre based youth work will not fit this model. The approach to club based work that I am advocating makes this clear. Youth workers are aiming to create an atmosphere where young people will associate with each other, enjoy themselves, work in groups together and have new experiences. It's quite easy to evaluate this visually, to survey young people, examine the notice boards etc., but if we have to set 'learning outcomes' we may find this more difficult.

The over-analysis of youth work has become as restrictive to club work as issue based work was in the 1980s. Of course workers should record their work, and this should be used in supervision where they can talk through their reflections, but the amount of paperwork full-time workers are being asked to produce is actually stopping them doing face-to-face work. Something Bamber (2000) called the Nightmare Scenario. See diagram below:

Bamber (2000: 9) suggests that 'the absence of any face-to-face work is a notable feature of what many practitioners will recognise as part of their daily reality'. His view is that the imposition of hierarchical and paper-based systems of management threatens to destroy youth works remit to pursue educational goals, which have been defined in voluntary association with young people.

In research into the impact of youth work Merton et al. (2005: 16) conclude that 'the risk is that the more that project work can demonstrate convincingly the outcomes of interventions, the more it feeds the decline of the work that cannot'. i.e. open access work.

Accreditation

Workers are now being asked to ensure that young people are accredited for participation in youth work (Resourcing Excellent Youth Work, 2002). The NYA (2003) have defined the difference between a contact and a participant, and, for the 15 per cent of young people who are participants, defined as 'active participation in a concentrated experience or at regular intervals over a period of time within a year', outcomes need to be recorded for 60 per cent of them. The IPPR report (Edwards and Hatch, 2003) feel that the focus on

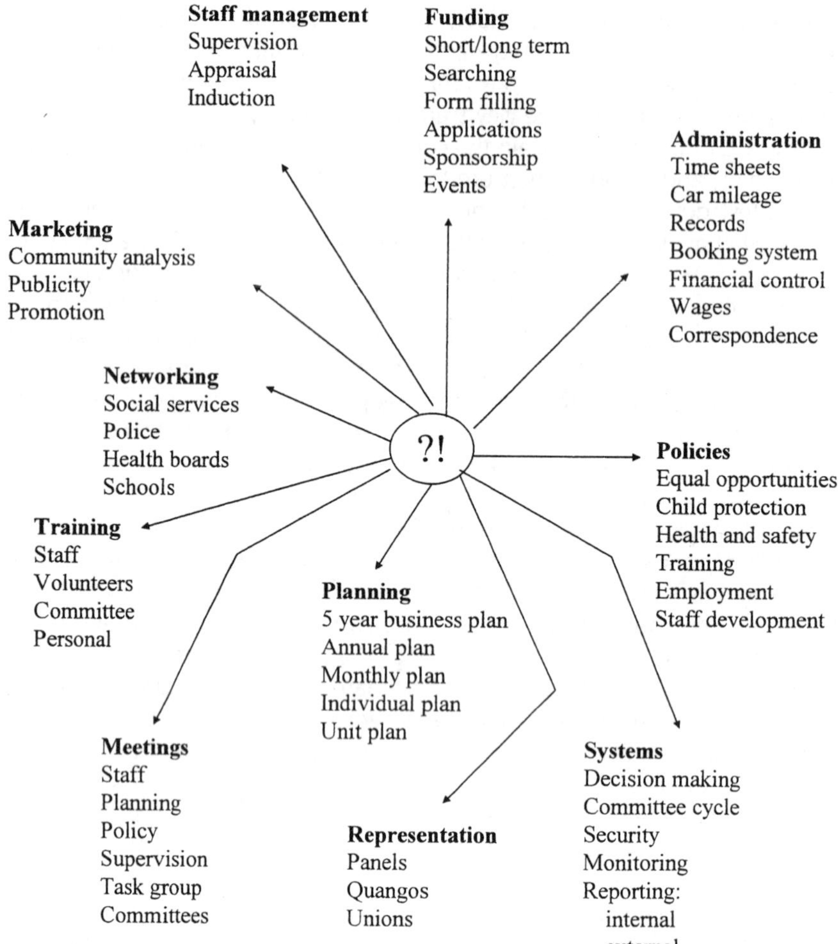

Figure 6.1 The nightmare scenario for youth work managers

accreditation in the youth service is too specific. They feel there is a danger that the process and accreditation is itself more important than the output, which should be a tangible impact on the lives of young people.

In 2001, Comprehensive Performance Assessment (CPA) was introduced for local authorities and this impacts on the work of the youth service. Councils are rated on key service delivery areas, including services for children and young people. An Audit Commission report (www.auditcommission.gov.uk) on the new approach to CPA, from 2005, looks to integrate inspections under the new children and young people agenda. Youth services are increasingly under scrutiny, the question is whether this has improved the work in youth clubs, which are central to the service.

If we accept that the abilities to motivate a group of young people, to organise a programme, to supervise a staff team and to liaise with other professionals, are important skills, then we have to let workers exercise them and support them in so doing. Fundamental to good practice must be supervision and support.

Throughout the country youth organisations, voluntary and statutory, have spent a great deal of time applying for SRB (Single Regeneration Budget) and other short term funding. Quick outcomes are demanded, with hard data, such as a fall in crime or better school attendance rather than soft data like making relationships with, or offering support to, young people. The youth service is being asked to work to an agenda which is focusing on a percentage of disaffected male young people – so that it is measured against other crime prevention methods – and probably found lacking. The youth service is not capable of offering a coherent programme to combat issues like crime, truancy, and alcohol abuse or youth unemployment. As Jeffs' stated as early as 1979, 'It is powerless to affect the root causes, so unfortunately it can rarely affect a cure' (Jeffs, 1979: 103). Marsland felt, in 1995, that the youth service was 'claiming absurdly more than was feasible'.

The national associations

Though not part of managing the service the two national associations provide support to workers and management committees in real and practical ways.

As we have seen, in Chapter 2, the first established national organisation for youth clubs was the National Organisation of Girls Clubs in 1911. The Girls Club Journal was established in 1912 and described the aims of the club in the phrase; 'After a long day's work what the girls most desire is some quiet place to sit in, which is cheerful and bright and warm'.

During the interwar years the Girls' Club Association began to admit young men and in 1944 it became known as the National Association of Girls Clubs and Mixed Clubs. In 1952 the order was changed, putting mixed clubs first, as the majority of the clubs had become mixed. By 1961 Girls had disappeared from the title and the Association became the National Association of Youth Clubs (NAYC). Carpenter and Young (1986) argue that 'the previously unquestioned validity of providing opportunities specifically for young women had finally slipped away'.

The National Organisation of Boys' Clubs was formed in the 1920s and both national organisations established local, usually county wide, organisations which could support local clubs. Clubs which affiliated over the years began to feel part of a larger organisation and to get support from fieldworkers, join in organised events, but also to benefit from insurance packages negotiated by the national organisations. They have been particularly useful to voluntary sector clubs with limited local authority support, and to small clubs which can rely on them to help programme activities with a calendar of events. They provide opportunities, not only for young people to meet together, but also for staff to meet other workers and to gain information and support.

The national organisations have sought national roles and often developed new work, as in political education and youth unemployment. In 1971 NAYC made funds available to help co-ordinate work with the young unemployed and brought together a working party which became the Standing Conference on Youth Unemployment. In 1971 it won a grant to run Community Industry which expanded during the early 1970s and led to NAYC being in receipt of the largest ever grant given to a voluntary youth organisation (Davies, 1999).

NAYC was also not afraid to develop new work in the area of girls' work, appointing a specialist worker in 1977 and starting a *Working with Girls* Newsletter. However, these radical ideas were not shared by the NABC who expelled Cheshire Association of Boys' Clubs in 1977, because it decided to re-form as a county federation and register all its members with NAYC. NABC also adopted an entrenched position on separate work with gay young people which exhibited an underlying homophobia which Davies (1999) suggests was less openly held by many other youth organisations and workers.

Davies (1999) suggests that the NABC's thinking on mixed clubs throughout the 1980s and into the 1990s was split between those who wanted to focus on the 'true boys' club' and those who wanted to see a change to its single sex policy. In 1994 NABC formally acknowledged the participation of girls in its affiliated clubs by changing its title to the National Association of Clubs for Young People (NACYP).

NAYC changed to Youth Clubs UK, perhaps to be seen as trendier, and then to UK Youth, losing any mention of clubs or youth work. Indeed, today UK Youth seems much more preoccupied with the training of young people than the traditional running of competitions and provision of resources for clubs. It is now the NACYP which fills that role, in West Sussex for example, although in some areas both organisations work together under one name, such as Young Gloucestershire. Clubs still look to the associations for insurance cover and practical support, many associations employ development workers to support their clubs. The Rural Youth Work Forum has also recently lost the 'work' part of youth work from its title to become Rural Youth. This generalising, and trying to cover all aspects of the lives of young people, is particularly true of the National Youth Agency.

The National Youth Agency

Following a government review of voluntary sector funding in 1989 there was a decision to merge the National Youth Bureau, with a research and publications role, with CETYCW, the national organisation responsible for the training of youth and community workers. The National Youth Agency was created from this merger in 1991 (see Chapter 2 and Davies, 1999). The Agency's functions were originally those of monitoring and evaluating training provision and curriculum development. This was seen by many in the field to be a government imposed body, which would not dare to argue with government dictates. Although some suggested it would be the government's 'Rottweiler' rather than its 'Poodle' (Davies, 1999) the then director affirmed that it would be a conduit of the service's views to ministers, rather than express its own.

In 1995, and following the failure to implement a core curriculum for the youth service, a government review suggested that the NYA was remote from the field and not sufficiently committed to the voluntary sector. The DfEE threatened to cut the National Youth Agency's role and its funding (Davies, 1999). In the end funding was taken over by the Council for Local Education Authorities with the DfEE supporting its publishing activities.

In the late 1990s the NYA involved itself in trying to influence national policy; including lobbying political parties and party conferences before the 1997 election, and that is nowadays one of its key roles. Its mission is:

> *To advance work with young people – in public, private, voluntary and community sectors – that promotes their social and personal development, their voice and influence and their engagement and inclusion.*
>
> (www.nya.org.uk)

This does not even mention youth work, let alone clubs. The directors' recent comment about those who argue for a practice rooted in 'informal and convivial work' as 'utopian and stuck in the past or even oppositionalist' (Smith, 2003; Wylie, YPN, 2003) seemed to indicate that youth clubs were part of the past, although recently the NYA produced magazine, *Young People Now*, has had more positive comments and articles about clubs. Youth club work needs a higher profile within the NYA, to highlight the need for association and participation among young people, and the need for resources to be directed towards building based work. After all, it is the bedrock of all youth work provision.

CYWU

The Community and Youth Workers Union was formed in 1937 and has long been an important source of support for youth workers, full and part-time and in both the voluntary and statutory sector. It has fought consistently to protect the JNC pay scale for workers and recently negotiated a new grading matrix which should take account of the responsibilities taken on by centre-based workers. It continues to try to improve working conditions, besides providing invaluable help for workers in dispute with their managers. No worker should be without a copy of the general secretary's handbook on employment practice and policies (Nicholls, 2002) which covers important issues for centre-based workers such as health and safety.

Chapter 7

The Youth Club in the Community

This chapter looks at the relationship of the youth club and its community; at buildings, the community's view of young people, the workers role in the community, rural youth work, village clubs, one night a week clubs, church clubs and holiday schemes as well as work with schools and inter-agency work.

In the 1920s Cambridgeshire developed community colleges designed to incorporate recreational facilities, further education, schooling and youth work. This initiative went on to be adopted in other areas, and after the advent of comprehensive schools in 1964, many more 'community schools' were born. In Scotland this became the setting for all youth work.

Community work impacted on youth work from the 1960s and 1970s with the arrival of 'Educational Priority Areas' and 'Community Development Projects'. The word 'community' tended to become the panacea for all social problems, a phenomenon still with us today. Following the Milson-Fairburn report of 1970 (see Chapter 2) there was an increased emphasis on young people being seen as part of the community, and the youth service became effectively hitched to the community bandwagon.

The building

A good youth club should be at the heart of its local community and be a focal point for all young people in the area, so that it can become a community of young people. Large youth and community centres also cater well for the needs of the community, almost from cradle to grave! Community centres, such as the one I worked at in Widnes, first welcome toddlers into the playgroup, then go on to run the 'after school club', for 5–8-year-olds and then the junior youth club and holiday schemes. As they grew older the young people moved on to the senior club, and many of them eventually used the centre for weddings and 18th birthday parties or just dropped in for a drink in our licensed bar. The major benefit for a youth worker is that they can really get to know the young people, build up long term relationships, offer them challenges and opportunities and see them grow and move on. The young people in Widnes could officially be in the senior club four nights a week and sometimes take part in additional weekend activities and residential. If they had left school and were out of work, meeting down at the centre still remained the focal point in the day. It is important that the building's identity, as a place for young people to meet, is maintained. Many youth centres lend themselves well to welcoming adult groups such as senior citizens clubs, education classes or badminton clubs. Representatives from these organisations on a members' committee or the management committee can help support the work with young people, but it is important that the top priority remains working with, and satisfying the needs of, young people. One of the problems for youth workers in developing work with community groups is that they need space, especially the playgroup, for storing things, and this may mean a restriction on the use of the building for young people. It may also mean that other user groups start to dictate what happens in the building. When the youth club produced art work for Halloween I had to cover bits of naked witches with stick on bats to pacify the playgroup! The space should feel friendly to young people. Young people become reliant on the youth club as a place to meet and will react strongly when there are threats to close it. Brent (2001) feels that place is more important for young people who do not have the resources to move away – for many young people the community is part of their identity and of their destiny. It is difficult for young people to travel, buses are often unavailable and parents unable or unwilling to provide lifts, the club is often one place they can walk or cycle to easily, as many clubs are situated on residential estates.

The community's view of young people

One of the main roles of youth workers is acting as a spokesperson for young people, advocating their needs, and being a go-between when relationships get difficult.

A recent controversy over a youth work charity (*The Guardian*, 29.01.03) highlighted the difficulties youth workers sometimes experience from other members of the community. Some 400 young people a week visit Kids Company which operates as a drop-in centre in South London. Many of them are very needy and are living rough, but residents have fought a long campaign to get the charity evicted as they say they 'fear for their safety'.

Brent (1997) explored the 'otherness' of young people and he feels that they 'have the weight of disreputableness loaded onto them' and are created as 'outsiders within', mainly by their association with problems of crime. A *Guardian* article likened young people on estates to *Lord of the Flies* gangs: apparently the presence of large numbers of young people is automatically a problem.

Examining this issue Coles et al. (2000) researching on 10 housing estates asked about the challenges presented by 10–16 year olds: there was a wide consensus that the biggest problem was posed by them 'hanging around', sometimes this culminated in criminal behaviour but often it was just perceived as a nuisance. On their part the young people felt that adults viewed them as lazy and purposeless and felt like living up to this and 'giving them grief'. A large and significant minority of residents would have wanted to get rid of the young people: Coles (2000) likens it to ethnic cleansing.

Youth workers are attempting to bridge a very real divide between young people and adults. This doesn't just happen in urban environments: in fact prejudice against young people hanging around is often worse in small towns or villages. For instance:

> *I just had to write to express my horror at the plan to inflict Seaton with a so-called youth café. I am unable to believe that sensible members of society can consider inflicting a small peaceful seaside town with such an unnecessary source of trouble.*
>
> (*Pullmans Weekly News and Advertiser*, 9.02.01)

and,

> *A group of residents compare the area to Beirut, because of the gangs of 'out-of-control youths'. 'Help us to beat yobs' screams the front cover of the local newspaper.*
>
> (*Young People Now*, 23rd–29th June 2004)

The recent introduction of Anti-Social Behaviour Orders and youth curfews illustrate this attitude perfectly. In the introduction to the Anti-Social Behaviour White Paper, the Home Secretary, David Blunkett, paints a negative picture of young people as a threat to others, referring to '*youth hanging around street corners intimidating the elderly*' (quoted in Edwards and Hatch, 2003). However, many young people feel very aggrieved at being constantly moved on when they feel they are just hanging around with friends having fun (Edwards and Hatch, 2003).

This view of young people is often disturbingly backed up by the youth service, becoming 'managers of young people'. For example, St Helens Youth Service has recently set up a 'rapid response team' (YPN, 7–13 July) to target 'flashpoint areas around the borough'. It will work with police, the community safety team, resident's associations and local council members to identify young people likely to cause problems. The head of youth service is quoted as being very positive about this project which has cost £100,000 in its initial year, the money coming from *Transforming Youth Work*. It seems that youth work is being transformed in this way and some youth workers are taking what might be seen as a policing role. This seems to be an example of the service losing sight of the essential qualities of youth work, and as Smith suggests, losing faith in what they are doing (Smith, 2001).

The message of youth provision must be about more than diverting young people away from criminal activities. The youth service must create activities for young people to provide them with opportunities and to have fun. It is also the case that facilities for young people play an important role in ensuring that neighbourhoods feel reassuring places for adults (Edwards and Hatch, 2003).

The worker in the community

If part-time workers and volunteers are drawn from the local area they can often relate to young people more easily and will be able to sustain a relationship with them outside the club environment. Merton et al. (2005: 53) suggest that 'the credibility of youth workers in young people's eyes very often derives from being close to the community and having insight and understanding of the young people they work with'. Holman (2000) feels that living locally, in his case actually *in* the project, enhanced the relationships that he and his team were able build with the community. His is an exceptional story but it certainly can help relationships to develop more quickly if conversations with young people can also take place outside club hours. For a youth worker it depends upon how much of your personal life you want everyone to know about, and how much you want your job to be 24 hours a day. It helps build good working relationships with adults in the community, if you live locally rather than being seen as someone who commutes in and out. Unfortunately this can lead to misdemeanours by young people becoming the youth worker's problem. Even in my village, where I ran a youth club one night a week, the garage proprietor rang me up one evening to say that some young people were trying to buy cigarettes and she thought they were under age: she wanted to know what to do about it! Many full-time workers wonder whether their work would benefit if they lived locally to their club: it's a fine line between being able to listen to the confidences of young people and knowing too much about your neighbours. In the end it comes down to a matter of personal choice (Smith, 1988).

Brent (2002) discusses the idea of the youth worker as 'the outsider-within'. Brent is employed in a poor area of Bristol, and discusses the dilemmas of his life as a youth worker there, and the resentment that local people often have towards 'outsiders'. During his day he moves through some very different worlds in Bristol; in the youth club, in the street, at the BBC and in the arts centre and feels that the strains of being 'an outsider within' are one of the daily issues he faces as a youth worker. There are dangers with the role: the worker could romanticise it as being a hero venturing into 'difficult communities' or they could develop co-dependency where they can seem to feed off other people's difficulties. A third possibility, particularly when working with young people, is that of taking on the role of insider and speaking out on their behalf. The worker may not be able to get away from being seen as a representative of the authority and a spy on those worked with. Lastly, if the worker becomes a total stranger they cease to have any empathy for those they work with. However, having articulated these dangers, Brent concludes that there are great strengths in the 'outsider within' role: of knowledge and relationships with those we work with.

Smith (1994) proposed another view of a youth club worker's role as that of a 'local educator', someone who is part of the network of relationships in everyday life, someone who uses local facilities and is greeted on the street by local people. Someone who could be described as having high social capital (Putnam, 2000, see Chapter 8). However, Bunt and Gargrave (1980) felt that part-time workers often offered a narrow view of life and therefore were not always good role models for young people. They also tended to 'want to get on with the job and not waste time on theoretical discussions'. However, it is important to encourage part-timers to train and to recruit those willing to do so, whilst ensuring that the theory taught is seen as being relevant to practice.

In her essay, *Youth Workers as Community Workers* Lacey (1987) highlights the misconception that youth workers work with young people and community workers with adults. She also suggests that youth workers working with staff call it supervision or support, but this could also be called community action. The skills and experience of being a member of a community are legitimate baggage for staff to have. There is potential for young people to be involved in community activities and campaigns and to begin to organise for themselves.

She also feels there is a lack of clarity around the workers role with community groups, and with those adults who use the centre, and whether this is seen as legitimate work. It is important that a club worker focuses on the needs of young people, but the achievement of these can often be helped by the community work and networking undertaken by the youth club workers. Young people need an advocate in their local community.

Rural youth clubs

Early youth organisations did not only exist in the towns, as some interesting research by Fabes and Skinner points out (2001). They discovered parish records showing the development of early forms of youth club work, including the fact that payments were made in 1790 to keep the boys from playing on a Sunday: keeping the children occupied during church time led to Sunday schools. They highlight the role of the Girls Friendly Society, described as 'the village girls club movement', which had nearly 1,500 branches and nearly 20,000 members by 1913 (Fabes and Skinner, 2001). A range of activities were offered to the girls. The churches were at the forefront of these early forms of youth club; the Girls Friendly Society, for example, being strongly non-conformist and teaching temperance.

During the Second World War, the expansion of youth clubs was not just restricted to urban areas. In June 1940 there were no clubs at all in one particular small rural area: three years later there were 25 (National Association of Girls' Clubs Annual Report, 1943). This was probably due to the evacuation of large numbers of children from the cities, and the billeting of troops in rural areas (Smith, 1988). Rural provision took a similar form to that in the cities in that it adopted a broadly social model, although provision was often only on one night a week.

However, in the post Albermarle period, the major focus of provision was on urban young people. Young Farmers' Clubs were the major providers of rural youth work provision, and usually catered for the more motivated young people. The Salter-Davis report of 1964 concluded that the basic needs of urban and rural young people were the same; it did however make some recommendations about staffing and support (Watson, 2001).

Davies (1999) states that questions about gaps in rural provision appeared in each decade of youth service history. By the 1970s, with the economic crisis, the focus was on urban young people and inner city estates, but evidence was gathered of deprivation and high unemployment in rural areas too.

It was suggested that the majority of youth club attendees gave up as soon as they left school (Davies, 1999).

The Thompson Report (1982) did address the issue and recognised that rural deprivation did indeed exist. The Rural Youth Work Education Project, run and funded by the NAYC in the early 1980s held a national conference on rural youth work which created a Campaign for Rural Youth, which lobbied for increased funding and recognition of the problems. Innovative projects, such as the introduction of peripatetic workers and mobile space provision in rural areas began during the 1980s (Banks, 1993).

In the 1990s Youth Clubs UK developed a project to enhance the skills of volunteers, the majority of them being rural youth workers, and a National Forum was launched in 1997. Some money was made available in 1994 through the government's Rural Challenge, but generally during the 1990s rural young people were still disadvantaged in provision terms compared to those in urban areas. The position in 1997 was marginally worse than at the start of the decade with 67 per cent of rural parishes having no youth club (Davies, 1999). In addition, problems such as drug use, that had traditionally been seen as urban in nature, were also evident in the country, but there was little advice or support available for these young people.

The definition of 'rural' is not precise, although the Department of the Environment defines a 'rural settlement' as one with less than 10,000 inhabitants. One fifth of the English population live in 'rural areas,' in environments ranging from isolated farms to market towns. Some are in employment and are relatively well off, but many others may have to depend purely upon seasonal work. The deprivation faced by young people in rural settings may be less obvious than in the towns, and they can be severely disadvantaged by a lack of access to facilities (Watson, 2001).

Youth provision

The lack of provision for young people in the countryside is greater than in towns, but, in response to the problem for villages like Gregson Lane in the Ribble valley (where the nearest youth club is eight miles away, there is no bus service and residents complain about young people being out in the street), the only idea the government seems to have come up with is to impose a curfew (*The Guardian*, 9.12.2000).

Village facilities, such as playgrounds, are not usually designed to cater for children over the age of 10. These young people are then often given a hard time just for 'hanging about' there and local adults will sometimes go to extremes to stop them:

> *A new playground has been designed without slides, climbing frames or play equipment because nearby residents were worried that older youths would hang around the site at night.*
>
> (Robertson, 2000)

'Teenage villages', often a simple shelter with some sort of seating, have been established in places like Exmouth (YPN, 12.2.03) but they are often opposed by local residents. Parish councils are often the first port of call for complaints about young people out in the villages, and while some are quite helpful, even funding a youth worker or club, many are not. In 1999, a guide was produced to help councils address local problems by seeking partnership support for dealing with the problems caused by young people (Streich, 1999) – a case of keeping them off the streets again?

The main issues for young people are isolation, identity and access (Phillips and Skinner, 1994). These are also issues for young people in urban areas but are exacerbated by the rural situation. Watson (2001) identifies two factors as important for the success of rural youth work; the availability of volunteers and well trained staff within small communities, and the response of young people. Young people usually respond well to provision, but finding staff is very difficult, especially anyone with training or youth work experience. This is where the involvement of local associations and support from the local authority can make all the difference.

Many different initiatives have been tried in rural areas – mobile projects, detached work, activity groups – but often young people simply want somewhere to meet. The National Youth Agencies pledge is to have premises within a bus ride of *all* young people, but in many country areas there are no buses. Some projects provide funding or access village transport from the county council: the Somerset Rural Youth Project for example has used minibuses to pick young people up and also runs an innovatory moped loan scheme. Otherwise parent's rotas – informal or organised by a youth worker can work well, parents in rural areas are very used to arranging lifts for younger kids, and it sometimes gets forgotten for older ones.

Village clubs

Village youth clubs are usually run on a one night a week basis and usually require a large commitment from adults to set up and supervise. The best way of improving the amount and quality of rural youth work would be to pay more attention to the needs of village clubs in terms of staffing, support and resources. Parish councils in some areas have been supportive, but young people are often not high on their list of priorities, and many residents do not want to pay for provision. There are funding mechanisms available such as the Groundwork Trust, the Lottery, SRB and the Countryside Agency, but accessing them is hard work for someone doing it on a voluntary part-time basis.

Those adults who work week in and out to run a village club deserve a medal. It's a thankless task and the local authority by and large does not support village clubs well. In some areas there will be a workers or leaders meeting which includes the leaders of part-time clubs. In some local authorities it may be the responsibility of a member of staff to keep an eye on the voluntary small clubs. But there is no overall strategic planning or vision, and if a club closes due to lack of adult help or premises, often no one has a role to try and resurrect it. One initiative in Somerset, the Somerset Rural Youth Project, filled this valuable role, and even got some parish councils to support the work. Young people were involved in small villages in making video films describing their situations – of a complete lack of youth provision. The local Associations of Youth Clubs help small clubs by providing insurance and activities for the clubs, and training and support for workers. Chester and Wirral Federation of Youth clubs used to have a regular leaders meeting which was valued as an important support for full and part-time club leaders. Many of the Associations also provide training and support with a worker to help local clubs get off the ground.

Generally small village clubs do not have their own premises, and meet in the village hall. This space is often used by other groups who are 'out to get the youth club'! I was once telephoned and asked to come and remove a cream egg from a keyhole, as one of the youth club had left it there the night before. Obviously it got missed in the final clear up, and it was impossible for the playgroup leader to remove it! At Christmas the youth club members were called vandals and worse when the paper chains came down: in shared buildings any damage will definitely be down to the youth club, and any trouble in the area too. The perception is that a youth club will encourage young people to hang about the village late at night when they should be safely at home watching television – sometimes they even smoke! The important thing for the worker is not to be sucked into this emotionally. Plenty of other groups hang about in villages – look at the pensioners outside the village shop and the mums outside the school! Young people have the right to some public space. Research conducted in several other countries (Dee, 2000) demonstrated that the perception of their use of space as bring problematic is not new, or solely confined to the UK.

An NAYC report of 1994 (Phillips and Skinner) found that young people in rural settings are more likely to attend or become members of youth organisations than their urban counterparts, which may be because there are fewer other options. Because they are only open one night a week village clubs often work with a larger age range than a town club would. The club needs to be sensitive to the needs of both younger and older members, and organise structured activities for the younger ones. In a small community the age issue is not so important, as the young people in a village rely on each other for company and haven't as many other friends to choose from as those in the city! However, the older young people often prefer to go to the larger club in the next village.

One-night-a-week clubs

The village club is the classic example of a one night a week club but such clubs also operate in urban areas where they are often run by tenants' organisations or groups of concerned parents. Many youth clubs meet, often only one night a week, in premises belonging to other organisations in the community such as schools, churches, and community centres. These clubs certainly need the support of their local communities to thrive. Other clubs are run by religious organisations: some of which are exclusive, i.e. only for Hindus whilst others may be open to anyone, even if they do not share the faith concerned. Local education authorities occasionally offer some full-time worker's or officer's support. A survey conducted in Croydon into the number of part-time clubs operating in the borough led to the appointment of an officer with a particular brief to support them. More often, however, clubs are left to get on with it: sometimes the local authority may not even be aware of their existence. With the increased emphasis on police checks for those working with young people, recruiting and supporting volunteers would be a valuable role for local authorities to perform. Currently the Criminal Records Bureau processes around 40,000 police checks a week, and there are long delays (YPN: 14–20, May 2003).

Church clubs

Since the beginning of youth work, churches of all denominations have been involved and have tried to undertake the dual role of serving not only their own members but also the other young people in the area. The Methodist Association of Youth Clubs, formed in 1945, has paid employees who support youth workers in affiliated clubs across the country, although their salaries are often paid by the local authority (Leighton, 1972). There are now 7,900 full-time paid youth workers employed by churches along with many thousands of volunteers (*Young People Now*, May 2003: 14–20). Membership of some church groups involves an element of worship; however, many workers see their role more as one of involving young people within the local community. The Gap in Herne Bay felt that there was a lack of provision for young people and '. . . want them to feel part of something and keep out of trouble' rather than aiming to convert them. Greene (1997) suggests that this whole area needs examination at a time when there is an increase of the work of the voluntary sector, with many new workers being appointed by religious organisations. She explores the three different approaches that can be adopted by workers in church projects; the informal education approach, the directive approach and the conversion approach. She suggests that a good youth worker, whatever their personal views, will use an informal education approach to help the young person come up with options for solving problems.

Holiday schemes

For many years youth clubs have run holiday schemes. Some are club holidays but others have an organised plan of activities for a two or three weeks period which young people can take part in during the day. It's a great opportunity for club workers to get involved in fun activities like canoeing or to organise large scale events, like taking 100 young people by train to walk to an island across the sand and bring them all back again before the tide comes in. Unfortunately, local authority youth services are often not prepared to subsidise these activities or even to allow staff to run them. This is a great shame, as existing members of the youth club benefit from these new experiences, new members are recruited, the older young people can get involved with helping the younger ones – and everyone, including staff, has fun.

Summer university projects have been set up by some London boroughs to provide activities for young people. The police noticed that crime drops significantly when there are summer activities going on and have started running, or at least funding, them under the banner of SPLASH for instance. Tracey Smith, the SPLASH Co-ordinator for Wiltshire said:

> *The idea behind SPLASH is to give young people something constructive to do during the long school summer holidays, instead of hanging around the streets getting bored or into trouble.*
>
> *SPLASH also gives young people the opportunity to try something new and meet new friends, while keeping them safe from harm. Keeping young people occupied relieves family tensions during this long difficult period, as well as helping to make our communities safer places.*
>
> (www.splashwiltshire)

The most recent initiative, launched in July 2003, replaced SPLASH by Positive Activities for Young People (PAYP) which offers exciting opportunities for young people in sport and the arts. Funding comes from Connexions, the National Lottery, the Home Office and the Youth Justice Board. The allocation of this money is based upon factors such as truancy rates and crime hotspots, and is targeted towards young people who are perceived to be 'at risk'. This is very much in line with the government's social exclusion agenda (see Chapter 8):

> *Young people get these activities in return for agreeing to go into education, training or employment.*
>
> (Ann Weinstock, Chief Executive of Connexions, quoted in YPN, July 2003)

The problem with some of these schemes though is their 'short termism' which makes recruiting staff and setting up the projects very difficult, also there is no overall strategy about how all these schemes fit together to improve young peoples lives in an area (Edwards and Hatch, 2003). They do not tackle the root cause of why some young people are excluded, unmotivated or at risk. The activities are not integrated with support and advice to tackle underlying problems. It would make more sense to use the existing facilities for young people i.e. youth clubs, so that the involvement could continue even when the holidays are over. These initiatives also only target young people who are already having difficulties in their lives, rather than being preventative, which a good youth club can be.

Work with schools

The Newsom Committee of 1963 had called for youth work approaches to be used in school with those of average or below average ability, and set a target date for an increase in the school leaving age. At that point, the leaving age of 14 meant that the Youth Service officially dealt with those over school leaving age. It was now felt that closer relationships should be developed with schools, and that schools should operate clubs. There was a steady growth in youth tutor posts and they amounted to some 20 per cent of appointments by the mid 1960s (Davies, 1999). Since these workers not only ran the youth club, but also taught in the school they needed to be qualified teachers. The number of youth work courses within teacher training expanded, and youth wings were constructed on school sites.

Davies (1999) suggests that while they were welcomed by some groups, such as Asian parents, the initiative was disliked by others, particularly the older teenagers who did not feel inclined to go back to school again in the evening. One major benefit was that the youth club gained access to a variety of valuable additional facilities such as use of the school gym, games courts, grounds and minibuses. However, the question of who manages the work, the youth service or the head teacher, is often difficult to resolve. Youth clubs on school sites are often held responsible for any vandalism on the premises, even on nights when the club is closed! The Coopers Lybrand Deloitte report of 1991 felt that, due to the introduction of local management of schools, there were opportunities for youth workers to become more involved in schools (Davies, 1999). However, with increasing emphasis on the financial viability of individual schools, it was felt that head teachers might well want to use the youth cub premises to generate money and would start to charge clubs for use of school facilities. Arrangements were worked out on a local basis and a 1992 NYA survey showed that the threat was only serious in a small minority of local authorities.

Throughout the 1990s the DfEE tried to use the potential of youth workers in schools, especially with 'disaffected' pupils. Many local authorities responded positively and youth workers started spending time in schools or running day time groups in youth centres, particularly under SRB schemes. By 1998, eighty three youth services were involved in work in schools (Youth Service Audit, NYA, 1998). With the advent of Connexions even more youth workers have become involved with schools. Research suggests that collaboration, however, has endemic problems arising from the different priorities of agencies and their differing definitions of 'need' (Tett, 2000). Youth workers may feel that the most difficult young people are being 'dumped' on them while teachers may feel that youth workers are 'too soft' on young people. An evaluation of the Gloucestershire Youth Action Scheme, which involved extensive collaborative working with schools, showed that co-operation often depended on the personal relationship that had been built up between the youth worker and the relevant school staff. Building these relationships (networking is the more technical term for it), is the bedrock of inter-agency work and co-operation. Many professionals have strongly stereotyped views of other specialists and this barrier can only be broken down by working together for the benefit of the young people.

Certainly, building relationships with the local schools, including special needs schools, is a vital part of a youth club worker's job. It is important, however, that youth workers do not become sucked into the school's own agenda: delivering personal and social education lessons may be a possible role for a youth worker, but it is easy to end up prioritising work in the school over work in the club. Working in a very structured way with a group of disaffected young people in school time is hard, but rewarding work, and this may contrast significantly with the nature of the relationship you develop with them in the informal setting of the club where school rules do not apply. Balancing the roles of teacher and youth worker is not easy, and the respective responsibilities need to be clearly agreed with the school. The reforms proposed by the *Every Child Matters* white paper (DfEE, 2003) include putting more youth services within schools. Youth workers in schools can be useful intermediaries in personality clashes with teachers (YPN 23–29th June 2004: 9) but this seems to be another example of youth work moving away from its core principles. The problem of pupil disaffection in schools should be solved by teachers in my view, not youth workers.

Edwards and Hatch (2003) felt that it would make sense to maximise the value of the capital resource of a school in an area, with its IT and arts equipment for example, but there are difficulties in using school locations for young people who are antagonistic to school or may be excluded from it. The government's Five Year Strategy for Children and Learners, published in July 2004 proposes 'extended' schools supplying support services for young people, this could be cheaper than having a separate service such as Connexions (Smith, 2004). Many schools see the value of having a youth wing on site and a school in Brighton has recently opened a 'drop-in' after school provision, to be staffed by Connexions advisors, youth workers and health workers. However, if youth clubs start becoming too much like school, one can only suspect that young people will vote with their feet.

Merton's 2005 research highlighted the need for greater clarity about the purpose of the work and its relationship with mainstream schooling.

Inter-agency Work

Apart from the youth workers, many other adults will be involved in the club on a full-time, part-time or voluntary basis; members of the management committee, parents, caretakers, cleaners, builders and decorators. Increasingly, youth workers are being asked to liaise with, take part in inter-agency meetings with, and work in partnership with their fellow professionals such as social workers, teachers and the police. For club workers the important thing is to build these local relationships, but a club worker should always be on and sometimes literally at, the young person's side. If a youth club member is up before the court, some input on how helpful they are around the club can really help and, of course, no young person should have to go to court alone. Informal lunches are often a good way of getting to know other workers in the area, and networking is an important skill for club workers to develop. Youth club workers also need to be in touch with their local community even if they do not actually live there. There are many ways for the youth club to get involved in local events, such as charity work or festivals, and take on community service, which can provide good positive publicity opportunities for the club in particular and young people in general.

As Young (1998) argues, social exclusion, disaffection and disadvantage are multi-faceted problems which need multi-faceted inter-agency responses. The youth service's involvement is a crucial part of its responsibility to young people, but the service must not lose its identity and principles in doing so. Marsland (1993) felt that the unprincipled chasing of money by the youth service was diluting youth work, and submerging it in the objectives, procedures and values of other services.

Inter-agency work became a major plank of government policy from the mid 1980s, and while all youth services may have been involved prior to that they had not necessarily taken the lead until the advent of the Youth Action Scheme in 1993. The YAS projects established inter-agency working and ranged from quite relaxed informal links to much more formal committees (France and Wiles, 1997). Youth work gained in status from taking on the lead role. Other more recent initiatives, such as the Youth Offending Teams and Connexions have seen youth work managers operating in many different inter-agency environments: the Connexions pilots, for example, were found to demonstrate how to do multi-agency work successfully (Dickenson, 2001). Youth services have always had the voluntary sector as a key partner and most have now formal service level agreements (SLAs) (Merton et al., 2005).

The government is concerned to get services working more closely together: in some local authorities, e.g. Brighton and Hove, the council are forming Children's Trusts to bring services together (YPN, July 2003) and these will be rolled out nationwide by 2008. The Minister for Children and Young People is in charge of developing a co-ordinated approach. It remains to be seen whether this initiative benefits young people or merely adds to bureaucracy.

Chapter 8

Conclusion: The Way Forward for Youth Clubs

Since the advent of the new Labour government, the political agenda has been dominated by the ideas of social exclusion. In this chapter I examine how this concept has determined policy towards the youth service. I feel that this concept, and that of social capital, could be used to argue for more youth club provision in the 21st century.

Social Exclusion

In the 1970s the term 'social exclusion' was unknown and indeed was absent from standard sociology textbooks of the 1990s (Haralambos and Holborn, 1991; Taylor, Richardson et al., 1995). However, social exclusion is at the centre of current social policy, replacing poverty as the concern of academics and politicians alike. There have been significant changes in the character of advanced industrial societies with the decline in the numbers of manual unskilled jobs in the labour market, and in particular in the youth labour market (Hayton, 1999). The Conservative Government after 1979 promoted the market as the sole organising principle of economy and society (Hutton, 1995) and inequality in Britain grew during the 1980s and 1990s, creating problems for social cohesion. A situation developed whereby 40 per cent of people held down relatively secure well paid jobs, 30 per cent were in insecure 'flexible' positions and 30 per cent were not in paid work at all (Hutton, 1995). Analyses such as this led to the concept of social exclusion, and how to tackle it.

The development of a new political language about social cohesion, stake holding, community, social exclusion and inclusion was central to the development of New Labour's ideas, and, after their election in 1997, led to the setting up of the Social Exclusion Unit located in the Cabinet Office. Levitas (1998) suggests that the government's agenda is narrow; concentrating on the importance of paid work as a way of decreasing spending on benefits, and not allowing for the importance of unpaid work, or indeed of leisure and community activities in helping people to become socially included. An insistence on the integrative role of employment pushed the concept of social exclusion away from ideas of social participation (Levitas, 1998).

Social participation

In this definition social exclusion is the result of actions taken by those who exclude – those who have power. For instance, the policy of some local authorities is to put single parents in hard-to-let housing on run down estates. Social exclusion is dynamic: it is the result of experience over time, and can be transmitted over generations. Social exclusion is not only about poverty, but also about deprivation and whether people are able to participate in community life (Alcock, 1999).

Most people are involved in all sorts of networks; social networks, political and civil networks, employment networks, community and family networks, voluntary sector networks, public services networks and private services networks. The truly socially excluded are involved in none of these, and could be said not to participate in society.

Young people

The 'problem of youth' is an old one – moral panics over youth movements such as 'teddy boys', 'skinheads' and 'rave' culture form the history of youth policy (Osgerby, 1998). Governments often react to an issue that affects only a small minority of young people, rather than considering the need for a long term, coherent youth policy. For example, Smith (1997) looks at the Albermarle Report of 1960 and the disturbances which occurred in Notting Hill and Nottingham in 1958 and increasing levels of juvenile crime. Albermarle reported that there was 'widespread and acute social concern'. Bloxham (1997) points out that a pattern of negative attitudes to young people is long-standing, for example the Thatcherite views that young people were in need of control and should not be entitled to live off the state. She suggests that many young people are truly on the margins of society and are excluded from participation in key aspects of mainstream society, mass youth unemployment in the 1980s created a spectre of unemployed and alienated young men who were seen as threatening the social order (Bloxham, 1997). Policies that introduced schemes such as the Youth Training Scheme were based on a deficiency model i.e. the problem was seen as a skills deficit in young people individually, rather than a lack of employment opportunities. It can be seen that these views of young people have carried on into policy initiatives today (Mizen, 2003). It is also the case that life chances for young people have become polarised between those who are doing OK, and those facing marginalisation and exclusion (Joseph Rowntree Foundation, 2002).

Young people from poor backgrounds face a 'poverty penalty,' and are not benefiting from the expansion of further and higher education.

How can youth clubs help?

The PAT12 report highlighted the problems of young people in the UK compared with those in other countries (Policy Action Team 12, 2000). This led to a cross-departmental unit for children and young people being set up in the DfEE. One issue highlighted in the report is the lack of safe, interesting and affordable leisure facilities for young people. It also suggests that young people can benefit enormously by participating in community and voluntary activities. Many youth workers believe youth club provision (*Young People Now*, September 2000; Smith, 2003) is at risk of disappearing, as the youth service becomes more focused and targeted around getting young people into work. It is undoubtedly true that young people need individual help and guidance, such as that offered by personal advisers as part of Connexions (DfEE, 2000) but they also need friendly adults to relate to and a warm, safe place to meet their friends. For social inclusion to become a reality its focus needs to be wider than concentrating just on paid work (Levitas, 1998).

Experience shows that a good youth club can provide valuable help for adolescents, and in particular, for those who would fall into the definition of 'socially excluded' and who would be likely to leave school with no qualifications. However, Williamson (1997) suggests that, while youth work provides social gathering places there is still pressure to present a good image which is best achieved by getting rid of trouble makers. My research suggests that these are often the same young people who have been excluded from school, or have excluded themselves. Youth service rhetoric on the other hand, declares that it prioritises work with these young people, but what it often does is set up or support separate projects for 'the disaffected' rather than providing the community provision that young people say they need.

Social capital

Putnams (2000) work on social capital has been influential in the development of UK policy on communities. I would argue that it can be used to support arguments for meeting places for young people – youth clubs.

Social capital refers to connections among individuals – social networks and the norms of reciprocity and trustworthiness that arise from them. 'It consists of the stock of active connections among people: the trust, mutual understanding, and shared values and behaviours that bind the members of human networks and communities together and make co-operative action possible' (Cohen and Prusak, 2001: 4) quoted in Putnam (2000).The concept implies that building community spirit and trust requires face-to-face encounters. In '*Bowling Alone*', Putnam (2000) argued that a decrease in associational activity in the United States since the 1960s had led to a decrease in 'social capital'. He feels that this is a problem, as social capital makes an enormous difference to our lives and allows people to resolve collective problems more easily. This work has been extensively critiqued (Field, 2003; Baron, Field and Schuller, 2000) as to whether this is really the case in America and whether it applies elsewhere. However, it's clear that social norms and networks provide a mechanism for ensuring that people do their share. It's difficult to refuse to bake a cake for the school fair when all the other mums are doing it, and they all know you – it's still possible, but you need a very good excuse! Social capital 'greases the wheels that allow communities to advance smoothly' and makes us behave better, 'people who have active and trusting connections to others develop or maintain character traits that are good for the rest of society'. Putnam (2000) feels that joiners are more tolerant and more empathetic to others misfortunes.

Networks

The networks that constitute social capital also help the flow of information in the community through informal gossip outside the shop, or down at the youth club. There is also evidence that having social capital is good for our health: people whose lives are rich in social capital cope better with traumas and fight illness more effectively. Putnam (2000) illustrates how important groups are for health:

> *As a rough rule of thumb, if you belong to no groups but decide to join one, you cut your risk of dying over the next year in half. If you smoke and belong to no groups, it's a toss-up statistically whether you should stop smoking or start joining.*
>
> (Putnam, 2000: 331)

Smoking has always been a diffficult issue in clubs. Will young people improve their health more if allowed in with their cigarettes than if they stopped smoking, but stayed outside?

Social connectness

Social connectness is very important for health and happiness – people nowadays may be *feeling* worse even though they are actually physically healthier. Putnam (2000) shows that, in the United States at least, public spaces are cleaner in high social-capital areas, people are friendlier, and the streets are safer. He links high crime rates to the fact that 'people don't participate in community organisations, don't supervise younger people, and aren't linked through networks of friends' (307–18). Young people rob and steal not only because they are poor, but also because adult networks and institutions have broken down. This is particularly true in disadvantaged neighbourhoods, and suggests that regeneration should be as much about encouraging the growth of social networks and safe places to meet as providing employment or improving housing. The opportunities and choices for young people, and hence their development, are affected positively by the networks that exist in their everyday lives and those of their parents. One of Putnam's findings was that young people in the 1990s have fewer, weaker and more fluid friendships than teenagers did in the 1950s.

Volunteers and community activists

Every community activist would recognise another of Putnam's main conclusions: if you want something done ask a busy person! This still doesn't answer the question of why some people get involved and others don't, is there a personality type for volunteering? It's certainly my impression that it is more difficult to get people involved in village committees, management committees, PTAs and so on than it used to be. Putnam (2000) used extensive research to show that the involvement of Americans in their community was down in every respect compared to 20 years ago. A highly civic generation had been replaced by others who were less so: each generation reaching adulthood since the 1950s was less engaged in community affairs than its predecessor. He called those born between 1965 and 1980 generation X and found them inwardly focused, materialistic and socially isolated. On average, American teenagers spend three and half hours alone each day.

Why?

Putnam attempted to explain this decline and the main culprit came out as television. 'A major commitment to television viewing is incompatible with a major commitment to community life' (Putnam, 2000: 229) however, this view has been criticised (Field, 2003) for instance and research has shown that young people still get most of their sex education from friends rather than TV (p99). Another interesting conclusion Putnam reached is that if you are the sort of person who switches on the TV when you enter a room, and surf the channels, you are not the sort of person to turn up at the PTA meeting. So, if you are looking for volunteers for your youth club, ask people about their viewing habits! He also found that commuting time was an important factor, with a 10 per cent increase in commuting time leading to 10 per cent less time spent on community activities. Commuting time in the UK is higher than in any other European country, and our working hours are longer. It should therefore come as no surprise to find that people have little time or energy left for their local community at the end of a long and busy day.

Bonding and bridging social capital

Putnam (2000) identifies two types of social capital, bonding and bridging. Bonding strengthens the links in communities while bridging attempts to make links between communities.

In 2001 there were racially motivated riots in Oldham, Burnley, Leeds and Bradford, mainly involving young people. The government commissioned a series of reports, the common theme of which was the lack of community cohesion – this was defined as 'requiring a shared sense of belonging, respect for differences and acceptance of reciprocal rights and obligations of community members' (Thomas, 2003). Research undertaken by Thomas (2003) into this concept with young people concluded that social capital had great relevance for community cohesiveness, particularly the idea of bridging social capital, which youth work should be involved in building (Merton et al., 2005).

How can youth clubs help?

Assuming that Putnam's findings are true to some extent in the UK, then one of the effects of a comparable decrease in social capital in the UK has been a decline in significance of youth clubs as a place to meet. The idea of social capital provides a powerful rationale for youth clubs – they are central to the generation of social capital within communities. The simple act of joining and being regularly involved has been shown to have a significant impact on health and well-being. This leads Smith (2001) to the conclusion that open and generic work needs a higher priority and 'issue based work needs to be interrogated as to the benefits it brings'. The Ritchie Report into the riots in Oldham was unequivocal on the value of youth clubs and felt that the falling away of traditional youth activities based on youth clubs had left a gap. They felt that the emphasis in youth clubs on formal social education, led to youth workers acting more like teachers and the alienation of many young people (Thomas, 2003). The report also felt the facilities available for young people were inadequate and called for new buildings.

Merton et al. (2005) found that youth workers make a distinctive contribution to social capital by prioritising work with groups of young people rather than concentrating on individuals and that the creation of social capital should be seen as the distinctive purpose of youth work. Where better to do this than in youth clubs?

New youth clubs

The government is concerned to build social capital (Field, 2003) so new places for young people to meet should fit current policy agendas.

In 1997 Bradford argued that youth work had never been able to colonise a distinct territory of its own and youth workers had been forced to occupy the spaces left by other institutions, such as social work or leisure. It is true that youth work has needed to develop its own intellectual and political space, but it does have a distinct physical territory of its own. Youth clubs are, after all, the place where youth workers work: they work in other places of course, but if you want to find a youth worker I suggest you try a youth club. Youth clubs give youth workers a haven and a locale that is 'uniquely their own' (Jeffs and Smith, 1993).

The IPPR report, Passing Time (Edwards and Hatch, 2003) looked at young people's view of their community and what they want to see provided out of school. It argues that 'providing good facilities and services for teenagers is vital for building strong communities that feel safe, vibrant and supportive for everyone'. They concluded there was a need for a national strategy to give young people modern, social, friendly spaces – modern youth clubs. They suggested calling them Young Clubs after Sir Michael Young. They feel that the facilities must be local, accessible and inclusive, involving young people in designing and running them. Without funding for clubs they conclude, 'We are in real danger of our kids coming to be looked on not as the future of community, but the death of it'.

Another recent initiative '51 Minutes', suggests that policy makers should be looking seriously at the use children and young people make of the 51 minutes in every hour they are not in school. The lack of safe play space for all ages is a major problem.

The most concerted effort to boost provision of modern spaces and youth clubs is the Make Space Campaign run by Kids club network with Nestlé Trust Funding. It aims to establish 3,000 Make Space out of school clubs by 2005. While this is to be applauded it is my view that the government and the community should be making this investment, particularly to avoid taking money from private sector companies like Nestlé. Many young people who have been involved in the baby milk campaign would agree. So, how can we persuade the government and local authorities to act?

A national strategy for youth clubs

Quality Develops, Towards Excellence in Youth Services (NYA, 2001) includes a Local Youth Pledge of Entitlement which could be used to shape local services and hold politicians accountable. The pledge includes 'a safe, warm, well equipped meeting place, within a bus ride, with facilities for drama, music, sport, voluntary action and international experience'.

In reply to a question on investment in the youth service Tony Blair said 'we have to invest in programmes – making sure that the youth services are properly funded so that young people have something to do and somewhere to go, rather than hanging about on street corners, creating mischief'.

This common stereotype of young people has been with us since the beginning of the industrial revolution, but the response to it then, the creation of youth clubs, seems to be eluding us today.

Two recent reports, the IPPR (Edwards and Hatch, 2003) and Ritchie (Thomas, 2003) highlight the need for new buildings, and any tour of any Local Authority's buildings will demonstrate it. One authority had not built a new club for over 40 years (Menton et al., 2005). However, Albermarle buildings can be transformed into something that young people will be happy to use today – especially if they have been involved in the design, as is happening in Portishead for example.

Recent work has been done on the cost of detached work (Crimmens, Factor et al., 2004). Extending street-based youth work to provide projects in the most deprived 5 per cent of areas in England and Wales would cost around £24 million a year. The report suggests that provision, covering the most deprived 50 per cent of areas, would cost around £142 million. This is about 4 per cent of the budgets in those areas for secondary schools and compares with £450 million a year currently spent on Connexions.

Calculation of the cost of bringing youth clubs up to scratch has been attempted in Wales. The Estyn Report (1999:18) *Adult Education and Youth Services*, noted that 'in the case of youth work, whilst there are notable exceptions, many buildings do not meet the need of contemporary youth provision or are poorly maintained'.

The report into the refurbishment and maintenance of buildings, undertaken by four local authorities, felt that the need for the refurbishment of existing premises was greater even than the need for new buildings. The report highlighted the kind of benefits which follow from improved facilities – increases, both in terms of numbers of young people which attended and, perhaps more importantly, in the average age of the young people. This demonstrated that young people respond to an environment which shows them that they are valued. Decent, properly equipped and furnished premises are respected by young people and suffer little or no vandalism.

The authorities represented in the report (Estyn, 1999) owned forty-four premises used for youth work. The vast majority of these were either very old (100 years or more) or built during the 1960s as part of the response to the Albermarle Report. Almost all were in very poor condition and getting progressively worse. The vast majority also lacked access for the disabled and raised serious health and safety concerns. Estimates for refurbishment were between £50,000 (for a small 'terrapin', de-mountable structure), to upwards of £200,000 for a larger property. The group felt that an average unit cost of £100,000 would be reasonable. That is, the cost of fully refurbishing all youth work premises in the principality could well be upwards of £20 million. This would, however, leave unaddressed the need for new facilities in areas where none exist at present. An equivalent exercise badly needs doing for England – there are 2,421 local authority youth service owned buildings (White, 2003) so at a similar average unit cost the total would be £250 million. A one off capital investment such as this could make a real difference and compares well with the cost of recent short term initiatives e.g. the budget for the Positive Activities Scheme is £25 million. However, these costing exercises are meaningless without the political will to implement change.

Learning from our history

As we saw earlier (Chapter 2), the history of youth clubs can be likened to a roller coaster. The question now is whether the journey will continue. A new pot of gold has appeared called Transforming Youth Work, the question now is, transformed it into what?

The argument, against concentrating resources on groups and individuals who present the strongest social problems can and must be made, if generic youth work, as described in these pages, is to be preserved. Putnam's (2000) work shows that crime can be reduced, educational achievement enhanced, and better health fostered, through the strengthening of social capital. Social capital can be strengthened by access to club and group life – not by focusing on the perpetrators and blaming the victims, but by improving the quality of community life and association for young people. Social exclusion does not have to be a reality for today's young people. Youth clubs can't solve all our social problems, but they can be a focus for young people to get together, to start to feel part of a community, and to think about how to change their lives for the better. The need for political education for young people has never been greater.

In the past the youth service has tried to face two ways, to respond to new demands, but also to keep its universal core provision, of open access traditional youth work i.e. clubs. This universal provision is increasingly under threat. The impact of youth work research (Merton et al., 2005) concluded that local authorities are finding it increasingly difficult to maintain a balance between open access and targeted work. They found that the different forms of provision are mutually supportive and that there are dangers in allowing open access work to decline. They felt that the evidence suggests open access work is important to maintain because it can identify young people who need more intensive support; it provides young people with wider networks and offers young people association and activity, hence contributing to key social policy objectives, as outlined in Every Child Matters (DfES, 2003: 117) of active citizenship, aspiration and achievement, enabling and protection. The dilemma between universalism and selectivity is one of the tensions and dilemmas highlighted by Davies (1999). It is the key one in the history of youth clubs. Of course, youth clubs were often built in areas of social need, which may have changed over the years, but were traditionally open to all young people of stipulated ages who chose to attend. The recent targeting of youth work on poor areas gives the message that youth work is only for deprived young people, who need special treatment. A good youth club needs a mixture of young people from its area, middle class young people need youth clubs just as much as working class ones. The ideal club provides an environment where people from different backgrounds can mix together and learn from each other.

The youth service needs to return to first principles. Before Connexions hit us, Young (1998) was arguing that we should 'stick to the knitting' meaning that the youth service should stay close to the business it knows. Young concludes that, in 1991, the youth service missed its chance to pursue and clearly articulate what the principles enshrined in the ministerial conference statement of empowerment, participation and equality of opportunity really mean in practice.

A return to those principles, even at this late stage, could help the service establish how it can best help young people in the transition from childhood to adulthood. Despite Jeffs and Smith's questioning of youth as a concept (1998) and of youth work as a profession, 'youth work is like whaling or lamplighting, no longer required', the latest government initiatives are concerned about youth as a category, and see a clear role for the youth service. Unfortunately, for many of us in the service, it is not a role that sits easily with our own principles. As Bunt and Gargrave affirmed in 1980 'the youth club approach to the social education of the young has played a part of major importance in the lives of young people in the past'. If it is to do so in the future a major injection of public money is needed to transform youth clubs into environments fit for the 21st century: where young people can come to meet their mates, get advice, engage in activities, plan events, organise themselves and make relationships with each other and with the adults involved. They shouldn't be huge drafty barns: they must be warm and comfortable and open when young people want to use them, with resources available such as computers, minibuses etc. There are some good examples around:

> *The Interchill project in Liverpool is an internet and drop in centre for young people. The money from it was raised by young people and they own the building and employ the worker.*
>
> (Edwards and Hatch, 2003)

A youth worker at the Emmanuel Project in London (YPN, 27.08.03: 12) said:

> *The way it has been designed and the layout is really excellent. It encourages young people to come in. If there were a lot of buildings like this, more young people would feel able come in, talk to their friends and relax.*

. . . and a young persons view:

> *You get to socialise with other people, meet new people, get advice, get to do things – it's fun.*

Youth clubs are places where youth work is done, and which young people attend voluntarily in their leisure time. Over the last few years the definition of youth work has been endlessly argued. Many youth workers today are involved in Connexions, youth justice and work with schools and excluded pupils. However, *Resourcing Excellent Youth Services* (DfES, 2002) sets out a list of youth work values, the first of which is 'young people choose to be involved, not least because they want to relax, meet friends and have fun'.

It also states that 'it takes place because young people are young people, not because they have been labelled or categorised as deviant'.

In my view, this vision of the youth service being complementary to the formal education service would best be achieved by supporting and enhancing the youth club provision which has been sorely neglected for far too long.

The need is not just for the present, because people remember their youth club experience and draw on it throughout their life:

> *The youth club was a social oasis, nothing else offered the opportunities the club did.*
>
> (Youth Council for Northern Ireland, 1998)

As a friend said to me recently:

> *You've reminded me how great the youth club was, what fun I had, what I got involved in, I'd really like my son to go to something like that – do they still exist?*

They do, but, like Tinkerbelle and the fairies, they will continue to do so only as long as people believe in them – and affirm that belief at all levels.

References

Acta (2002) *At Home on the Slopes. A History of Hartcliffe and Withywood.* Bristol: ACTA.

Alcock, P. (1999) Lecture given at West Midlands Regional Social Policy Conference.

Ashby, L. (2001) Working with Lesbian, Gay and Bisexual Young People. In *RHP Companion to Working with Young People.* Lyme Regis: Russell House Publishing.

Ballard, D. and Wright, S. (1994) *Research Project on Centre Based Work.* Gloucestershire Youth Service.

Bamber, J. (2000) Managing Youth Work in Scotland. *Youth and Policy.* 68: 5–18.

Banks, S. (1993) Community Youth Work. In Butcher, H., Glen, A., Henderson, P. and Smith, J. (Eds.) *Community and Public Policy.* London: Pluto.

Banks, S. (1999) *Ethical Issues in Youth Work.* London: Routledge.

Baron, S., Field, J. and Schuller, T. (2000) *Social Capital.* Oxford: Oxford University Press.

Batsleer, J. (1996) *Working with Girls and Young Women in Community Settings.* Aldershot: Arena.

Berne, E. (1972) *Games People Play.* London: Pan.

Birkett, D. (2001) Don't Lock the Kids up: Let Them Out. *The Guardian.* 02.08.01.

Blandy, M. (1967) *Razor Edge: The Story of a Youth Club.* London: Gollancz.

Bloxham, S. (1993) Managerialism in Youth and Community Work. *Youth and Policy.* 41: 1–12.

Bloxham, S. (1997) The Social Contract Between Young People and Society. In Kendra, N. and Ledgerwood, I. (Eds.) *The Challenge of the Future.* Lyme Regis: Russell House Publishing.

Bolger, S. and Scott, D. (1984) *Starting from Strengths*. Leicester: National Youth Bureau.

Booton, F. (1985) *Studies in Social Education. Vol. 1, 1860–1890.* Hove: Benfield Press.

Bourn, D. (2003) Global Perspectives in Youth Work. *Youth and Policy.* 80: 6–22.

Boyle, J. (1977) *A Sense of Freedom.* London: Pan.

Bradford, S. (1997) The Management of Growing up: Youth Work in Community Settings. In Roche, J. and Tucker, S. (Eds.) *Youth in Society*. Open University: Sage Publications.

Bradford, S. (2000) Disciplining Practices: New Ways of Making Youth Workers Accountable. *International Journal of Adolescence and Youth.* 9: 45–63.

Bradford, S (2004) The Value of Youth Work to the People That Matter. Clubs for Young People.

Bradford, S. and Day, M. (1991) *Youth Service Management.* Leicester: Youth Work Press.

Brent, J. (1997) Community Without Unity. In Hoggett, P. (Ed.) *Contested Communities.* Bristol: Policy Press.
Brent, J. (2001) Trouble and Tribes. *Youth and Policy.* 73: 1–19.
Brent, J. (2002) Crossing Worlds: The Youth Worker as Outsider-within. *Youth and Policy.* 77: 1–18.
Brew, J (1943) *In the Service of Youth.* London: Faber.
Brew, J (1947) *Youth and Youth Groups.* London: Faber.
Bunt, J. and Gargrave, (1980) *The Politics of Youth Clubs.* Leicester: National Youth Bureau.
Button, L (1971) *Discovery and Experience.* London: Oxford University Press.
Button, L. (1974) *Developmental Group Work with Adolescents.* London: Hodder and Stoughton.
Button, L. (1975) *Developmental Group Work in the Youth Organisation.* Leicester; NYB.
Button, L (1981) *Group Tutoring for the Form Teacher; I, Upper Secondary.* London: Hodder and Stoughton.
Byrne, D. (1999) *Social Exclusion*. Buckingham: Open University Press.
Carpenter, V. and Young, K. (1986) *Coming in From the Margins.* Leicester: NAYC.
Chauhan, V. (1987) *Beyond Steel Bands and Samosas.* Leicester: NYB.
Cilliers, P. (1998) *Complexity and Postmodernism.* London: Routledge.
Cohen, P. (1997) *Rethinking the Youth Question: Education, Labour and Cultural Studies.* London: Macmillan.
Coleman, J. and Hendry, L. (1990) *The Nature of Adolescence*. London: Routledge.
Coleman, J. and Warren-Adamson, C. (1992) *Youth Policy in the 1990s. The Way Forward.* London: Routledge.
Coles, B. (1995) *Youth and Social Policy: Youth Citizenship and Young Careers.* London: University College of London Press.
Coles, B., England, J. and Rugg, J. (2000) 'Spaced Out? Young People on Social Housing Estates. *Journal of Youth Studies.* 3: 1, 21–33.
Cotterell, J. (1996) Social Networks and Social Influences. *Adolescence*.
Coward, R. (2001) Hogwarts, the Haven. *The Guardian.* May 20th.
Crimmens, D., Factor, F. et al. (2004) *Reaching Socially Excluded Young People: A National Study of Street-Based Youth Work.* Leicester: Joseph Rowntree Foundation/NYA.
CYWU (1994) *Planning for a Sufficient Youth Service.* CYWU.
CYWU (2000) *PAT 12, Young People*. Conference delegates briefing paper. CYWU.
Davies, B. and Gibson, A. (1967) *The Social Education of the Adolescent.* London: University of London Press.
Davies, B. (1999) *A History of the Youth Service in England*. Volumes One and Two. Leicester: Youth Work Press.
Dee, M. (2000) No Hiding Place. *Young People Now.* April 20–21.
DES (1969) *Youth and Community Work in the 70s. Proposals by the Youth Service Development Council.* (The 'Fairbairn-Milson Report') London: HMSO.
DES (1983) *Young People in the 80s: A Survey.* London: HMSO.
DES (1987) *Effective Youth Work. A Report by HM Inspectors. Education Observed 6.* London: DES.

DES (1989) *Changing Attitudes: The Youth Service and Young People.* National Advisory Council for the Youth Service.
DES (1990) *Youth Work with Black Young People*. London: HMSO.
DES (1995) *Young Peoples Participation in the Youth Service.* Statistical Bulletin.
Dewey, J. *The Encyclopaedia of Informal Education.* http://www.infed.org/thinkers/et-dewey.htm
DfE (1994) *Inspecting Youth Services.* HMSO.
DfEE (1999) *Moving on up, How Youth Work Raises Achievement and Promotes Social Inclusion.* Leicester: NYA.
DfEE (2000) *Connexions, the Best Start in Life For Every Young Person.* London: Nottingham: DfEE.
DfEE (2001) *Transforming Youth Work.* Nottingham: DfEE.
DfEE (2003) *Youth Work Planning for the Local Authority Youth Service 2003–2004*. Nottingham: DfEE.
DfES (1982) *Experience and Participation: Report of the Review Group on the Youth Service in England*. (The Thompson Report) London: HMSO.
DfES (2002) *Transforming Youth Work, Resourcing Excellent Youth Services.* London: DfES/Connexions.
DfES (2003) *Every Child Matters.* London: The Stationery Office.
DfES (2005) *The Impact of Youth Work.* London: The Stationery Office.
Dickens, C. (1853) *Bleak House*. Harmondsworth: Penguin Books.
Dickenson, P. (2001) *Lessons Learnt from the Connexions Pilots.* London: DfES.
Disraeli, B. (1845) *Sybil.* Harmondsworth: Penguin Books.
Eager, W. McGregor (1953) *Making Men.* London: University of London Press.
Edwards, L. and Hatch, B. (2003) *Passing Time.* London: Institute for Public Policy Research.
Eggleston, J. (1976) *Adolescence and Community.* London: Edward Arnold.
Estyn Report (1999) *Adult Education and Youth Services*. Cardiff: National Assembly of Wales.
Evans, W. (1965) *Young People in Society.* Oxford: Basil Blackwell.
Fabes, R. and Skinnner, A. (2001) The Girls Friendly Society and the Development of Rural Youth Work 1850–1900. In Gilchrist, R., Jeffs, T. and Spence. J. *Essays in the History of Youth and Community Work.* Leicester: Youth Work Press.
Factor, F., Chauhan, V. and Pitts, J. (2001) *The RHP Companion to Working With Young People.* Lyme Regis: Russell House Publishing.
Field, J. (2003) *Social Capital.* London: Routledge.
Foreman, A. (1987) Youth Workers as Redcoats. In Jeffs, T. and Smith, M. (Eds.) *Youth Work*. London: Macmillan Education.
France, A. and Wiles, P. (1997) The Youth Action Scheme and the Future of Youth Work. *Youth and Policy.* 57: 1–15.
Furlong, A. and Cartmel, F. (1970) *Evaluating Youth Work with Vulnerable Young People.* Research report No. 83. Edinburgh: SCRE.
Gauthier, A.H. and Furstenberg, F.F. (2001) Inequalities in the Use of Time by Children and Young Adults. In Vleminckx, K. and Smeeding, T.M. (Eds.) *Child Wellbeing, Child Poverty and Child Policy in Modern Nations.* Bristol: Policy Press.
Ghose, D. (2002) Youth Work Needs You. *Young People Now.* 12.2.02.

Gilchrist, A. (1999) *Community Networks.* IACD Conference Paper.
Gilchrist, A. (2004) *The Well Connected Community.* Bristol: Policy Press.
Goldman, R. (1969) *Angry Adolescents.* London: Routledge and Kegan Paul.
Greene, M. (1997) A Religious Perspective for Youth Work. In Ledgerwood, I. and Kendra, N. (Eds.) *The Challenge of the Future.* Lyme Regis: Russell House Publishing.
Griffen, C. (1993) *Representations of Youth.* Cambridge: Polity Press.
Haralambos, M. and Holborn, M. (1991) *Sociology: Themes and Perspectives.* London: Collins.
Hayton, A. (Ed.) (1999) *Tackling Disaffection and Social Exclusion.* London: Kogan.
Heath, S.B. and McLaughlin, M.W. (Eds.) (1993) *Identity and Inner-City Youth. Beyond Ethnicity and Gender.* New York: Teachers College Press.
Heller, N. (2003) Lord of the Flies Gangs Rule Estates. *The Guardian.* 17.08.03.
Henriques, B. (1933) *Club Leadership.* London: Oxford University Press.
Henriques, B. (1951) *Club Leadership Today.* London: Oxford University Press.
Hendry, L., Shucksmith, J., Love, J. and Glendenning, A. (1993) *Young People's Leisure and Lifestyles.* London: Routledge.
Holden, S. (1989) *Youth and Policy.* August, 27.
Hollin, C. (1987) *Just a Phase? Essays on Adolescence.* Leicester: Youth Clubs UK.
Holman, B. (2000) *Kids at the Door Revisited.* Lyme Regis: Russell House Publishing.
Holmes, J. (1981) *Professionalisation: A Misleading Myth?* Leicester: NYB.
Holmes, J. (1997) Youth Work: Time for Another Government Review? *Youth and Policy.* 57: 29–39.
Huskins, J. (1996) *Quality Work With Young People.* Bristol: Huskins.
Hutton, W. (1995) *The State We're In.* London: Jonathan Cape.
Ingram, G. and Harris, J. (2001) *Delivering Good Youth Work.* Lyme Regis: Russell House Publishing.
Jeffs, A. (1979) *Young People and the Youth Service.* London: Routledge and Kegan Paul.
Jeffs, T. (1997) Changing Their Ways: Youthwork and 'Underclass' Theory. In Macdonald, R. (Ed.) *Youth, the Underclass and Social Exclusion.* London: Routledge.
Jeffs, T. (2003) Self-esteem: the Costs and Causes of Low Self-Worth. By Nicholas Elmer. Feature review *Youth and Policy.* 28: 69–76.
Jeffs, T. (2004) Basil Henriques and the House of Friendship. In Gilchrist, R., Jeffs, T. and Spencer, J. (Eds.) *Architects of Change: Studies in the History of Community and Youth Work.* Leicester: Youth Work Press.
Jeffs, T. and Smith, M. (1990) *Young People, Inequality and Youth Work.* London: Macmillan Education.
Jeffs, T. and Smith, M. (1998) The Problem of 'Youth' for Youth Work. *Youth and Policy.* 62: 45–65.
Jeffs, T. and Smith, M. (1999) *Informal Education.* 2nd edn. Ticknall: Education Now Books.
Jeffs, T. and Smith, M. (1999) Resourcing Youth Work; Dirty Hands and Tainted Money. In Banks, S. (Ed.) *Ethical Issues in Youth Work.*
Jeffs, T. and Smith, M. (Eds.) (1988) *The Promise of Management for Youth Work: Young People, Inequality and Youth Work.* London: Macmillan Education.
Jeffs, T. and Smith, M. (Eds.) (1989) Taking Issue with Issues. *Youth and Policy.* November 28.

Jenkinson, H. (2002) The Importance of being Supervised. *Young People Now.* 161: September 08–28.

John, G. (1981) *In the Service of Black Youth.* Leicester: NAYC.

Joseph Rowntree Foundation (2001) *Young Peoples Changing Routes to Independence.* www.jrf.org.uk

Joseph Rowntree Foundation (2002) *Disabled Teenagers Experience of Access to Inclusive Leisure*. www.jrf.org.uk

Joseph Rowntree Foundation (2002) *Disaffected Youth in Multi-cultural Areas.* www.jrf.org.uk

Joseph Rowntree Foundation (2003) *Urban Regeneration: Responding to Young People's Needs*. www.jrf.org.uk

Kealy, L. (1988) The Social Condition of Young People and Youth Work. *Youth and Policy.* 25: 6–18.

Klein, J. (1956) *The Study of Groups.* London: Routledge and Kegan Paul.

Kutner, J. and Factor, F. (2001) Inclusive Practice: Disability. In *The RHP Companion to Working with Young People*. Lyme Regis: Russell House Publishing.

Lacey, F. (1980) Youth Work in the Community. In Jeffs, T. and Smith, M. (Eds.) *Youth Work*. London: Macmillan Education.

Lacey, F. (1987) Youth Workers as Community Workers. In Jeffs, T. and Smith, M. (Eds.) *Youth Work*. London: Macmillan.

Leigh, M. and Smart, A. (1985) *Interpreting the Emerging Crisis of Purpose in Social Education.* Leicester: NYB.

Leighton, J. (1972) *The Principles and Practice of Youth and Community Work.* London: Chester House Publications.

Levitas, R. (1998) *The Inclusive Society?* London: Macmillan.

Lewin, K. (1948) *Resolving Social Conflicts.* London: Harper and Brothers.

Lewis, J. (2001) www.nya.org.uk

Lippett, R. and White, R. (1960) Leader Behaviour and Member Reaction in Three 'Social climates'. In Cartwright, D. and Zander, A. *Group Dynmaics.* New York: Harper and Row.

Lloyd, T. (1985) *Work with Boys.* Leicester: NYB.

Macdonald, R. (Ed.) (1997) *Youth, the 'Underclass' and Social Exclusion.* London: Routledge.

Marken, M. and Perrett, J. (1998) *England's Youth Service. The 1998 Audit*. Leicester: NYA.

Marsland, D. (1993) *Understanding Youth: Issues and Methods in Social Education.* St Albans: The Claridge Press.

Menton, B. et al. (2005) *An Evaluation of the Impact of Youth Work in England.* Research report No. 606. Nottingham: DfES Publications.

Milson, F. (1973) *An Introduction to Group Work Skill.* London: Routledge and Kegan Paul.

Ministry of Education (1961) *Bulletin 20: Youth Service Building: General Mixed Clubs.* London: Ministry of Education.

Ministry of Education (1963) *Bulletin 22: Youth Club, Withywood, Bristol.* London: Ministry of Education.

Ministry of Education (1960) *The Youth Service in England and Wales. The Albermarle Report*. London: HMSO.

Mizen, P. (2003) Tomorrow's Future or Signs of a Misspent Youth? Youth Policy and the Blair Government. *Youth and Policy.* 79: 1–18.

Mugger (1990) *The New Statesman*. 9.11.90

Murray, C. (1990) *The Emerging British Underclass.* London: Institute of Economic Affairs.

Myhill, S. (1985) *Youth Clubs.* Leicester: NAYC.

National Association of Girls Clubs (1943) *Annual Report 1943.* London: National Association of Girls Clubs.

NACYS (1989) *Directions for the Youth Service: A Position Paper.* DES.

NAYC (1989) *Youth Work that Works.* Leicester: NAYC.

Newman, E. and Ingram, G. *The Youth Work Curriculum.* Further Education Unit.

Nicholls, D. (2002) *Employment Practice and Policies in Youth Community and Play Work.* 2nd edn. Lyme Regis: Russell House Publishing.

NYA (1995) *Planning the Way: Guidelines for Developing Your Youth Work Curriculum.* Leicester: NYA.

NYA (1996) *Agenda for a Generation.* Leicester: NYA.

NYS (2001) *Quality Develops Towards Excellence in Youth Services.* Leicester: NYA.

NYA (2003) The *National Framework of Awards in Non-formal Educational Settings.* Leicester: NYA.

NYA (2003) *Local Authority Youth Service Operational Planning 2004–05: Good Practice Guidance.* Leicester: NYA.

NYB (1990) *Danger or Opportunity: Towards a Core Curriculum for the Youth Service?* Leicester: NYB.

Ofsted (2000) Bristol Youth Service Inspection Report (www.ofsted.gov.uk)

Ofsted (2001) *Inspecting Youth Work: A Revised Framework for Inspection.* London: Ofsted/DfSS.

Ofsted (2002) Local Authority Youth Services and National Voluntary Youth Organisations. Ofsted (www.ofsted.gov.uk)

Ord, J. (2004) The Youth Service Curriculum and the Transforming Youth Work Agenda. *Youth and Policy* 83: 43–60.

Osgerby, B. (1998) *Youth in Britain since 1945.* Oxford: Blackwells.

Parsons, C. (1999) *Education, Exclusion and Citizenship.* London: Routledge.

Pelham, T.H.W. (1889) *Handbook to Youths' Institutes and Working Boys' Clubs.* London: London Diocesan Council for the Welfare of Young Men.

Phillips, D. and Skinner, A. (1994) *Nothing Ever Happens Around Here. Developing Work With Young People in Rural Areas;* Leicester: Youth Work Press.

Policy Unit, National Assembly for Wales (2000) *Extending Entitlement: Supporting Young People in Wales.*

Putnam, R. (2000) *Bowling Alone.* New York: Simon and Shuster.

Richards, W. (1995) Working With Mixed Race Young People. *Youth and Policy.* 49: 62–72.

Richardson, J. (1997) The Path to Adulthood and the Failure of Youth Work. In Ledgerwood, I. and Kendra, N. (Eds.) *The Challenge of the Future*. Lyme Regis: Russell House Publishing.

Riley, P. (2001) Programme Planning. In Deer Richardson, L. and Wolfe, M. (Eds.) *Principles and Practice of Informal Education.* London: Routledge Falmer.

Ritchie, D. (2001) *One Oldham, One Future.* London: Home Office.

Roberts, (1997) Is There an Emerging British Underclass? In Macdonald R. (Ed.) *Youth 'the Underclass' and Social Exclusion*. London: Routledge.
Robertson, S. (2000) Unpublished MA thesis. University of the West of England.
Robertson, S. (2000) A Warm Safe Space. *Youth and Policy*. 70: 71–8.
Robertson, S. (2001) Health Promotion in Youth Work Settings. In Orme, J. and Scriven, A. (Eds.) *Health Promotion, Professional Perspectives.* 2nd edn. Basingstoke: Palgrave.
Robertson, S. (2005) The Youth Service Curriculum. *Youth Policy*. 84.
Rose, C. (1998) *Touching Lives.* Leicester: Youth Work Press.
Rosseter, B. (1987) Youth Workers as Educators. In Jeffs, T. and Smith, M. (Eds.) *Youth Work*. London: Macmillan Education.
Rowntree Inquiry (1995) Joseph Rowntree Foundation. www.jrf.org.uk
Russell, C.E.B. and Rigby, L.N. (1908) *Working Lad's Clubs.* London: Macmillan.
Saffran Foer, J. (2003) *Everything is Illuminated.* London: Penguin Books.
SEU (1999) *Bridging the Gap.* London: The Stationery Office.
SEU (2000) *Young People: Report of Policy Action Team 12.* London: The Stationery Office.
Sennett, R. (1977) *The Fall of Public Man.* New York: Norton.
Sewell, L. (1966) *Looking at Youth Clubs*. London: NAYC. http://www.infed.org/archives/nayc/sewelllooking.htm
Sharpe, R. (2004) *The Withywood Experiment.* Private publication available from tricia&sharpesolutions.com.
Shaw, M. (2003) Connexions Should be Accountable for Every Penny. *Young People Now.* 2–8 July 8.
Singh Gill, B. (2001) Work with Boys and Young Men. In *The RHP Companion to Working with Young People.* Lyme Regis: Russell House Publishing.
Smith, A. (1994) *Creative Outdoor Work with Young People.* Lyme Regis: Russell House Publishing.
Smith, D. (1989) *Taking Shape; Developments in Youth Service Policy and Provision.* Leicester: NYB.
Smith, D. (1997) The Eternal Triangle: Youth Work, the Youth Problem and Social Policy. In Ledgerwood, I. and Kendra, N. (Eds.) *The Challenge of the Future*. Lyme Regis: Russell House Publishing.
Smith, H. (2002) Seeking out the Gift of Authenticity. *Youth and Policy.* 77: Autumn, 19–32.
Smith, M.K. (1980) *Creators not Consumers.* Leicester: NAYC.
Smith, M.K. (1988) *Developing Youth Work. Informal Education, Mutual Aid and Popular Practice.* Milton Keynes: Open University Press.
Smith, M.K. (1994) *Local Education.* Buckingham: Open University Press.
Smith, M.K. (2001) *Transforming Youth Work.* www.infed.org/youthwork/transforming_youth_work
Smith, M.K. (2001) *Young People, Informal Education and Association.* Paper compiled for Young People and Informal Education Conference, Strathclyde Sept, www.infed.org.uk
Smith, M.K. (2001) Youth Work and Informal Education. In Gilchrist, R., Jeffs, T. and Spence, J. (Eds.) *Essays in the History of Youth and Community Work.* Leicester: Youth Work Press.

Smith, M.K. (2002) *Transforming Youth Work, Resourcing Excellent Youth Services: A Critique*. the informal education homepage. www.infed.org/youthwork/transforming_youth_work_2.htm.

Smith, M.K. (2003) From Youth Work to Youth Development. The New Government Framework for English Youth Services. *Youth and Policy*. 79: 46–60.

Smith, M.K. (2004) *What Future for Youth Work? The English Five Year Strategy for Children and Learners*. The encyclopaedia of informal education, www.infeed.org/youthwork/five-year-stragy.htm

Social Exclusion Unit (2000) Young People-Policy Action Team Report 12. London: Office of the Deputy Prime Minister.

Solly, H. (1862) *Working Men's Clubs and Educational Institutes.* London: Working Men's Clubs and Institute Union.

Spence, J. (1988) Youth Work and Gender. In Jeffs, T. and Smith, M. (Eds.) *Young People, Inequality and Youth Work.* London: Macmillan Education.

Spence, J. (2001) Edwardian Boys and Labour in the East End of Sunderland: Welfare and Work. In Gilchrist, R., Jeffs, T. and Spence, J. *Essays in the History of Youth and Community Work.* Leicester: Youth Work Press.

Spence, J. (2001) Activities. In Deer Richardson, L. and Wolfe, M. (Eds.) *Principles and Practice of Informal Education.* London: Routledge Falmer.

Spencer, J., Tuxfors, J. and Dennis, N. (1964) *Stress and Release in an Urban Estate.* London: Tavistock.

Spender, D. (1980) *Man Made Language.* London: Routledge and Kegan Paul.

Standing Conference of Youth Organisations in Northern Ireland (1987) *Social Education in Practice.* Northern Ireland Youth Workers Association publication.

Stanley, M. (1890) Clubs for Working Girls. In Booton, F. (Ed.) (1985) *Studies in Social Education 1860–1890.* Hove: Benfield Press,

Stannard, D. (2000) Take Four. *Young People Now.* April 2000, 33.

Stead, D. (1992) *Facing Facts, The Future Delivery of Local Youth Services.* Leicester: NYA.

Steward, J. (2001) Work with Girls and Young Women. In *The RHP Companion to Working with Young People.* Lyme Regis: Russell House Publishing.

Streich, L. (1999) *Alternatives to the Bus Shelter: Imaginative Ways to make it Happen for Young People in Rural Areas.* Leicester: Youth Work Press.

Streich, L. and Howell, C. and Spafford, J. (1999) *Preventing Homelessness in the Countryside: What Works.* Cheltenham: The Countryside Agency.

Taylor, A. (2003) *Responding to Adolescents.* Lyme Regis: Russell House Publishing.

Taylor, P., Richardson J., Yeo, A., Marsh, I., Trobe, K. and Pilkington, A. (1995) *Sociology in Focus*. Ormskirk: Causeway Press.

Taylor, T. (1987) Youth Workers as Character Builders: Constructing a Socialist Alternative. In Jeffs, T. and Smith, M. (Eds.) *Youth Work.* London: Macmillan Education.

Tett, L. (2000) Working in Partnership. *Youth and Policy.* 68: Summer.

Thomas, P. (2003) Young People, Community Cohesion and the Role of Youth Work in Building Social Capital. *Youth and Policy.* 81: Autumn.

Truman, J. and Brent, J. (1995) *Alive and Kicking, the Life and Times of Southmead Youth Centre.* Bristol: Redcliffe Press.

Turnbull, A.M. (2001) Gendering Young People: Work, Leisure and Girls Clubs. In Gilchrist, R., Jeffs, T. and Spence, J. *Essays in the History of Youth and Community Work.* Leicester: Youth Work Press.

Ward, P. (1996) *Growing Up Evangelical: Youthwork and the Making of a Subculture.* London: SPCK.

Watson, J. (2001) Youth Work with Young People in Rural Areas. In *The RHP Companion to Working with Young People.* Lyme Regis: Russell House Publishing.

Webb, M. (2001) Black Young People. In Factor, F., Chauhan, V. and Pitts, J. (Eds.) *The RHP Companion to Working With Young People.* Lyme Regis: Russell House Publishing.

Webb, S. (2001) Some Considerations on the Validity of Evidence-Based Practice in Social Work. *British Journal of Social Work.* 31: 57–79.

Wheal, A. (1998) *Adolesence.* Lyme Regis: Russell House Publishing.

White, P. (2002) Steamed up About Self-esteem. *Young People Now.* 162 October, 24.

White, P. (2003) The Place for Me. *Young People Now.* 199 August, 12–4.

Williams, P.J (1993) *The Alchemy of Race and Rights.* London: Virago.

Williamson, H. et al. (1997) *The Needs of Young People aged 15–19 and the Youth Work Response.* Caerphilly: University of Wales and Wales Youth Agency.

Williamson, H. (1997) So What for Young People. In Ledgerwood, I. and Kendra, N. (Eds.) *The Challenge of the Future.* Lyme Regis: Russell House Publishing.

Willis, P. (1985) *The Social Condition of Young People in Wolverhampton in 1984.* Wolverhampton: Wolverhampton Borough Council.

Wylie, T. (2003) In and Against the State. *Young People Now.* 19th March, 20.

Wylie, T. (2004) How Connexions Came to Terms With Youth Work. *Youth and Policy.* 83: 19–29.

Wylie, T. and Merton, B. (2002) *Towards a Contemporary Curriculum.* Leicester: NYA.

Young People Now (2001) In the Neighbourhood. *Young People Now.* January, 28–9.

Young, K. (1998) Sticking to the Knitting. *Youth and Policy.* 60, Summer.

Young, K. (1999) *The Art of Youth Work.* Lyme Regis: Russell House Publishing.

Youth Clubs UK (1999) *Foundations.* Leicester: Youth Clubs UK.

Youth Council for Northern Ireland (1998) *Benefits of the Youth Service.* Belfast: Youth Council for Northern Ireland.